THE TEN PERCENT SOLUTION

Also from DARE BOOKS

Before the Setting Sun

Black Mother Goose Book

Dana the Procrastinator

Monica Made Me Promise

Ruff Poems, from the Heart

The Game of Life and How to Play It

The Magical Fountain of Love

The Secret Door to Success

The Struggle for Liberation

Wisdom in the Air, Wisdom Everywhere

Your Word Is Your Wand

The Ten Percent Solution

The Emancipation and Development of the African American Community

Desmond A. Reid

Published by
DARE BOOKS
Orlando, FL

Library of Congress Cataloging-in-Publication Data

Reid, Desmond A.
The ten percent solution: the emancipation and development of the African American community / Desmond A. Reid
p. cm.
Includes bibliographical references.
ISBN 978-0-912444-43-7 (pbk)--ISBN 978-0-912444-48-2 (hc)
1. African Americans—Social conditions. 2. Blacks—Social conditions. 3. Racism. I. Title
E185.86.R388 2010
305.896'073—dc22
2010028145

PRINTED IN THE UNITED STATES OF AMERICA

Contents

Preface

This book is written in an attempt to guide the most misguided group—the African American—on a path to self-sufficiency and happiness, which has, heretofore, eluded us. The intention is not to lambaste any other group. It's not about them! However, where the paths intercept (whether positively or negatively), the issues will be dealt with in an honest, forthright way, without regard to those who might register their denials.

There is no assumption that any group is monolithic. The contrary is true. However, there are certain *modus operandi* that are similar in the varied groups and so, any postulation here deals with the general perceived feelings and actions of particular groups. For example, when we speak of White people being racist, we recognize that there are some exceptions. Likewise, when we speak of the impossibility of impartial dialogue with Jews, we know that not all invoke anti-Semitism to answer all criticisms.

We also recognize that not all Blacks are open to discussion of the share of the blame we must bear for our dire condition throughout the world because it might be easier to blame others for our lack of success. It is even more difficult to consider the thought of treating some Blacks as our enemies (even more dangerous to us than the Ku Klux Klan) and to excise them.

We must be careful not to allow those who now seem inclined, to place a chasm between Africans and Latinos, as well as other "minorities" in their efforts to divide and conquer.

We must also recognize the bond between Africans in the Motherland and those in the diaspora, and get away from the regional thought of "who is better" and who does not belong.

We need to define our own leaders and allies, rather than have others do it for us, and we need to re-organize in constructive ways.

If we do what is proposed in these pages, not only will the Black population of the United States of America benefit, but the whole United States population, as well as the whole world will be enriched by the residuals. It is a fact that the Black man cannot sow any seed, anywhere, from which the White man does not reap fruit.

Furthermore, many studies have shown—over the years—that Whites live about eight years longer than Blacks and have a much better quality of life. These statistics are significant! However, the explanation to this lies in the fact that Black people are under constant stress, and stress kills (high blood pressure, heart attack, strokes, cancer, etc.). Empowerment reduces stress and increases joy, thereby adding to longevity. So, adhering to the principles postulated in this tome is a matter of life and death, both for the individual and the community.

For those who may say we do not have the answers or that others have tried some of the proffered tactics, we have but to answer that most of our readers may not have been exposed to those former ideas. Or that they might now be ready to explore other avenues! Whatever the case, since the problem has not been resolved, we need this other voice "crying in the wilderness."

There have been those who say this author seems angry and the answer is, "Yes, I am!" But it is a controlled anger toward both the victimizers and the victims—the victimizers for their cruelty and the victims for their far less than thought-out responses to their lot.

Dr. Kenneth Clark has written an article in the *New York Times* in which he said, "...any Black person who is not angry is not mentally well. In poor Black communities today where police kill Black men and youth with impunity the anger is still there and should be. It is a sign of good mental health. The real issue is what should Black people do to channel the anger to achieve justice."

This is what the author is trying to encourage.

This is a tell-it-like-it-is book. No holds barred, no apologies made!

Introduction

More than one hundred years after the end of chattel slavery in the United States, the African-America citizen of this country is still a slave. What is more, every African, everywhere is, to a lesser or greater extent, also a victim of the European slave system.

The tragedy of the whole situation is that the slave is, everyday, asking his slave master to set him free, instead of taking his emancipation into his own hands. He has not learned the lessons of the past.

Adam Clayton Powell, Jr. once asked, "What's in your hands?" The answer is, "Your destiny." One cannot ask a person or group of persons to act against its own self-interest. One has only to look at the history of the past thousand, or so, years to understand that it is in the self-interest of the caucasian population to keep the "colored" people away from the sources of power. The theory is that if you teach a man to fish, he becomes independent of you, while, if you give him fish, you can regulate the amount that you give to him and keep him dependent. Furthermore, if he is taught the art of fishing, he may end up catching bigger and better fish than you do. So he might be better fed!

The African communities in Africa and around the world (the diaspora) have, for many centuries, welcomed outsiders, only to have them come in and pillage and rape these communities. They have welcomed strangers and given them aid and comfort, only to have them steal the gold, the women and the heritage, and starve and murder their hosts.

They have saved their guests from death and enslavement, only to be killed and enslaved by these guests, and still they have not learned not to depend on them. They have not practiced the system of reciprocity referred to by Armah in his book, *Two Thousand Seasons.*

Slavery has been especially harsh in the United States, and Mr. Willie Lynch's edict of "divide and conquer" has been effective beyond expectation. It is the whip that lashes the horse one hundred and forty-plus years after the so-called emancipation of the American chattel slave. African Americans have remained burdened with the chain shackled tightly to their psyche as they continue to serve their master, while destroying themselves and their community.

Those who are not as tightly duty-bound to the master, nevertheless, expend so much time and energy in blaming the latter for their failure, that they cannot find the vision to, themselves, break the shackles. They have been "lynched," as was predicted by one of the presumed masterminds of the successful slave system, Willie Lynch.

Following is the text of what is presented as Willie Lynch's speech to American Slave and Plantation Owners in the year 1712 (courtesy of Black Arcade Liberation Library/ Transatlantic Productions, 1970):

Gentlemen:

I greet you here on the bank of the James River in the year of our Lord one thousand seven hundred and twelve. First, I shall thank you the Gentlemen of the colony of Virginia for bringing me here.

I am here to help you solve some of your problems with slaves. Your invitation reached me on my modest plantation in the West Indies where I have experimented with some of the newest and still the oldest methods for control of slaves. Ancient Rome would envy us if my program is implemented. As our boat sailed south of the James River, named for our illustrious King, whose version of the Bible we cherish, I saw enough to know that your problem is not unique. While Rome used cords of wood as crosses for standing human bodies along its old highway in great numbers, you are here using the tree and rope on occasion.

I caught a whiff of a dead slave hanging from a tree a couple of miles back. You are not only losing valuable stock by hanging, you are having uprisings, slaves are running away, your crops are sometimes left in the field too long for maximum profit, and you suffer occasional fires. Your animals are killed. Gentlemen, you know what your problems are; I do not need to elaborate, I am not here to enumerate your problems, I am here to introduce you to a method of solving them.

In my bag here, I have a foolproof method for controlling your nigger slaves. I guarantee every one of you that if installed correctly, it will control the slaves for at least 300 years. My methods are simple and any member of your family or overseer can use them.

I have outlined a number of differences among the slaves, and I take these differences and make them bigger. I use fear, distrust, and envy for control purposes. These methods have worked on my modest plantation in the West Indies and they will work throughout the South. Take this simple little list of differences; think about them. On top of my list is *"age"* but it is there only because it starts with an "a." The second is *color* or shade. There is intelligence, size, sex, size of plantation, status of plantation, attitude of owner, whether the slave lives in the valley, on the hill, East, West, North or South, has fine or coarse hair, or is tall or short. Now that you have a list of differences, I shall give you an outline of action—but before that I shall assure you that distrust is stronger than trust and envy is stronger than adulation, respect or admiration.

The nigger slave, after receiving this indoctrination, shall carry on and will become self-refueling and self-generating for hundreds of years—maybe thousands.

Don't forget that you must pitch the old nigger slave vs. the young nigger slave, and the young nigger slave against the old nigger slave. You must use the light skin slaves vs. the dark skin slaves and the dark skin slaves vs. the light skin slaves. You must use the male vs. the female and the female vs. the male. You must also have your white servants and overseers distrust all niggers, but it is necessary that your slaves trust and depend on us. They must love, respect, and trust only us.

Gentlemen, these kits are our keys to control—use them. Have your wives and children use them. Never miss an opportunity. My plan is guaranteed, and the good thing about this plan is that, if used intensely for one year, the slaves themselves will remain perpetually distrustful (of each other).

Thank you Gentlemen,
Willie Lynch

Acting on Willie Lynch's advice, the plantation owners and other slavers did a good job of making a slave, using the following recipe:

THE ORIGIN AND DEVELOPMENT OF A SOCIAL BEING CALLED THE NEGRO

Let us make a slave. What do we need? First of all we need a black nigger man, a pregnant nigger woman and her nigger boy. Second, we will use the same basic principle that we use in breaking a horse, combined with some more sustaining factors.

What we do with horses is that we break them from one form of life to another; that is, we reduce them from their natural state of nature. Whereas nature provides them with the natural capacity to take care of their needs and the needs of their offspring, we break that natural string of independence from them, and thereby create a dependency state, so that we may be able to get from them useful production for our business and pleasure.

For fear that our future generations may not understand the principle of breaking both horses and men, we lay down the art. For, if we are to sustain our basic economy we must break and tie both of the beasts together: the nigger and the horse. We understand that short-range planning in economics results in periodic economic chaos; so that, to avoid turmoil in the economy, it requires us to have breadth and depth in long-range, comprehensive planning, articulating both skill and sharp perception.

We lay down the following principles for long-range, comprehensive, economic planning:

1. Both horse and nigger are no good to the economy in the wild or natural state.

2. Both must be broken and tied together for orderly production.

3. For orderly futures, special and particular attention must be paid to the female and the young offspring.

4. Both must be crossbred to produce a variety and division of labor.

5. Both must be taught to respond to a peculiar new language.

6. Psychological and physical instruction of containment must be created for both.

We hold the above six cardinal principles as truths to be self-evident, based on the following discourse concerning the economics of breaking and tying the horse and the nigger together—all inclusive of the six principles laid down above.

Note: Neither principle alone will suffice for good economics. All principles must be employed for orderly good of the nation.

Accordingly, both a wild horse and a wild or natural nigger is dangerous even if captured, for they will have the tendency to seek their customary freedom and, in doing so, might kill you in your sleep. You cannot rest. They sleep while you are awake and are awake while you are asleep. They are dangerous near the family house and it requires too much labor to watch them away from the house. Above all you cannot get them to work in the natural state. Hence, both the horse and the nigger must be broken; that is, break them from one form of mental life to another—*keep the body and take the mind.*

In other words, break the will to resist. Now the breaking process is the same for both the horse and the nigger, only slightly varying, in degrees. But as we said before, there is an art in long range economic planning. You must keep your eye and thought on the female and the offspring of the horse and the nigger.

A discourse in offspring development will shed light on the key to sound economic principles. Pay very little attention to the generation of original breaking but *concentrate on future generations.* Therefore, if you break the female mother, she will break the offspring in its early years of development and, when the offspring is old enough to work, she will deliver it up to you for her normal female protective tendencies will have been lost in the original breaking process.

For example, take the case of the wild stud horse, a female horse and an already infant horse and compare the breaking process with two captured nigger males in their normal state, a pregnant nigger woman with her offspring. Take the stud horse, break him for limited containment. Completely break the female horse until she becomes very gentle whereby you or anybody can ride her in comfort. Breed the mare and the stud until you have the desired offspring. Then you can turn the stud to freedom until you need him again. Train the *female horse whereby she will eat out of your hand, and she will,* in turn train the infant to eat out of your hand, also.

When it comes to breaking the uncivilized nigger, use the same process, but vary the degree and step up the pressure so as to do a complete reversal of the mind. Take the meanest and most restless nigger, strip him of his clothes in front of the remaining male niggers, the female, and the nigger infant, tar and feather him. Tie each leg to a different horse, faced in opposite directions, set him afire and beat both horses to pull him apart in front of the remaining niggers. The next step is to take a bull whip and beat the remaining nigger she will beat her male to the point of death in front of the female and the infant. Don't kill him but put *the fear of God in him,* for he can be useful for future breeding.

The Breaking Process of the African Woman. Then take the female. Run a series of tests on her to see if she will submit to your desires willingly. Test her in every way because she is the most important factor in good economics. If she shows any sign of resistance in submitting completely to your will, do not hesitate to use the bull whip on her to extract that last bit of bitch out of her. Take care not to kill her for, in doing so, you spoil good economics. When in complete submission, she will train her offspring in the early years to submit to labor when they become of age.

Understanding is the best thing. Therefore, we shall go deeper into this area of the subject matter concerning what we have produced here in this breaking process of the female nigger. We have reversed the relationships. In her natural uncivilized state she would have a strong dependence on the uncivilized nigger male, and she would have a limited protective tendency toward her independent male offspring and would raise the female offspring to be dependent like her. Nature had provided for this kind of balance.

We reversed nature by burning and pulling one civilized nigger apart and bull whipping the other to the point of death—all in her presence. By her being left alone, unprotected, with the male image destroyed, the ordeal caused her to move from her psychological dependent state to a *frozen independent state,* In this frozen psychological state of independence she will raise her male and female offspring in reversed roles.

For fear of the *young male's life,* she will psychologically train him to be mentally weak and dependent but physically strong. Because she has become psychologically independent, she will train her female off-springs to be psychologically independent. What have you got? You've got the nigger woman out front and the nigger man behind and scared. This is a perfect situation for sound sleep and economics.

Before the breaking process, we had to be alertly on guard at all times. Now we can sleep soundly, for out of frozen fear, *his woman stands guard for us.* He cannot get past her early infant slave molding process. *He is a good tool, now ready to be tied to the horse at a tender age.*

By the time a nigger boy reaches the age of sixteen, he is soundly broken in and ready for a long life of sound and efficient work and the reproduction of a unit of good labor force.

Continually,—through the breaking of uncivilized savage niggers; by throwing the nigger female savage into a frozen psychological state of independence; by killing off the protective male image; and by creating a submissive dependent mind of the nigger male savage--we have created an orbiting cycle that turns on its own axis forever, unless a phenomenon occurs and re-shifts the positions of the male and female savages. We show what we mean by example. Take the case of two economic slave units and examine them closely:

The Negro Marriage Unit. We breed two nigger males with two nigger females. Then we take the nigger males away from them and keep them moving and working. Say the one nigger female bears a nigger female and the other bears a nigger male. Both nigger females, being without the influence of the nigger male image, frozen with an independent psychology, will raise their offspring into reverse positions. The one with the female offspring will teach her to be like herself, independent and negotiable (we negotiate with her, through her, by her, and negotiate her at will).

The one with the nigger male offspring, she being frozen with the subconscious fear for his life, will raise him to be mentally dependent and weak, but physically strong—in other words, body over mind. Now, in a few years when these two offspring become fertile for early reproduction, we will mate and breed them and continue the cycle. That is good, sound, and long-range comprehensive planning.

Warning: Possible Interloping Negatives. Earlier, we talked about the non-economic good of the horse and the nigger in their wild or natural state and we talked about the principle of breaking and tying them together for orderly production. Furthermore, we talked about paying particular attention to the female savage and her offspring, for orderly future planning. Then, more recently we stated that, by reversing the positions of the male and the female savages, we had created an orbiting cycle that turns on its own axis forever, unless phenomenon occurred and re-shifted the positions of the male and the female savages.

Our experts warned us about the possibility of this phenomenon occurring, for they say that the mind has a strong drive to correct and re-correct itself over a period of time if it can touch some substantial original historical base. They advised us that the best way to deal with this phenomenon is to shave off the brute's mental history and create a multiplicity of phenomena of illusions, so that each illusion will twirl in its own orbit, something similar to floating balls in a vacuum. The participation of a multiplicity of phenomena of illusions entails the principles of cross-breeding the nigger and the horse as we stated above--the purpose of which is to create diversified division of labor and different values of illusion at each connecting level of labor--the results of which is the severance of the points of original beginnings for each sphere illusion.

Since we feel that the subject matter may get more complicated as we proceed in laying down our economic plan concerning the purpose, reason, and effect of cross-breeding horses and niggers, we shall lay down the following definitional terms for future generations:

1. Orbiting cycle means a thing turning in a given path.

2. Axis means upon which or around which a body turns.

3. Phenomenon means something beyond ordinary conception which inspires awe and wonder.

4. Multiplicity means a great number.

5. Sphere means a globe.

6. Cross-breeding a horse means taking a horse and breeding it with an ass and you get a dumb backward ass long-headed mule that is not reproductive nor productive by itself.

7. Cross-breeding niggers means taking so many drops of good white blood and putting them into as many nigger women as possible, varying the drops by the various tones you want, and then letting them breed with each other until the circle of colors appear as you desire.

What this means is this: Put the niggers and the horse in the breeding pot, mix some asses and some good white blood and what do you get? You got a multiplicity of colors of ass backward, unusual niggers, running, tied to backward ass long-headed mules, the one productive of itself, the other sterile. (The one constant, the other dying—we keep the nigger constant for we may replace the mule with another tool) both mule and nigger tied to each other, neither knowing where the other came from and neither productive for itself, nor without each other.

Controlled Language. Cross-breeding completed, for further severance from their original beginning, we must *completely annihilate the mother tongue* of both the new nigger and the new mule and institute a new language that involves the new life's work for both. You know, language is a peculiar institution. It leads to the heart of a people. The more a foreigner knows about the language of another country, the more he is able to move through all levels of that society.

Therefore, if the foreigner is an enemy of another country, to the extent that he knows the body of the language, to that extent is the country vulnerable to attack or invasion of a foreign culture. For example, you take a slave—if you teach him all about your language, he will know all your secrets, and he is then no more a slave, for you can't fool him any longer, and *being a fool is one of the basic ingredients* of and to *the maintenance of the slavery system.*

For example, if you told a slave that he must perform in getting out "our crops" and he knows the language well, he would know that "our crops" didn't mean "our" crops, and the slavery system would break down, for he would relate on the basis of what "our crops" really meant. So you have to be careful in setting up the new language for the slave would soon be in your house, talking to you as "man to man" and that is death to our economic system. In addition, the definition of words or terms are only a minute part of the process. Values are created and transported by communication through the body of the language. A total society has many interconnected value systems. All these values in the society have bridges of language to connect them for orderly working in the society. But for these language bridges, these many value systems

> would sharply clash and cause internal strife or civil war, the degree of the conflict being determined by the magnitude of the issues or relative opposing strength in whatever form.
>
> For example, if you put a slave in a hog pen and train him to live there, and incorporate in him to value it as a way of life completely, the biggest problem you would have out of him is that he would worry you about provision to keep the hog pen clean--or partially clean--or he might not worry you at all. On the other hand, if you put this same slave in the same hog pen and make a slip and incorporate something in his language whereby he comes to value a house more than he does his hog pen, you got a problem.

The "community" decries the fact that every other ethnic group enters its borders, sets up businesses, becomes rich and moves out, leaving the empty slot for the next "invader." The self-same invader controls the institutions by becoming the "elected officials", the "educators" and the "civil servants."

The African American community complains all the way to the polling stations to elect these "leaders" or stays at home and allow them to be elected. They allow these educators to mis-educate their children, while they complain that the curriculum does not include the contributions of their people and, therefore, does not empower their children.

They complain about lack of respect and courtesy they get from the civil servants. Yet they don't make sure that these people do not get employment in these areas by preparing themselves to serve in these capacities, and having the right people in places so as to hire them and their relatives.

They complain about the police, but they don't prepare themselves to become policemen. Nor do they fight to overturn laws, such as that in New York City, which is unconstitutional, in that it bars New York City from requiring residency of its uniformed employees, while allowing the rest of the state to have such restrictions.

The law says that "cities of over a million population are enjoined from demanding residency" and since New York City is the only city in New York of over one million, the citizens of the city are treated differently from those of the rest of the state, which is unconstitutional.

The result is that they get policemen, from the suburbs, who do not know or respect residents of the Black community. They regard them as "fodder for prisons," mistreat and kill them on the streets like wild animals. These uniformed personnel also earn money in the city while spending it and paying taxes in other areas. Thus, the city does not benefit from the residuals of this employment.

If the African American fails to act immediately and decisively, the cry will be the same one hundred years from now, two hundred years from now, and one thousand years from now.

In spite, and maybe because of, the election of an African-American president of the United States, it will not become easier for Black people in this world. Two things are happening which will stymie our progress. The first is that this occurrence has hackled the ire of the ultra-racists and they have begun to redouble their efforts to stop us. By the bullet, if necessary! The second thing is that, in the minds of many humanitarians, we have now entered the post-racial era, and all racism has been wiped out. In their minds, the playing field has been leveled, so there is no need for further protagonism.

The problem is so enormous that it tends to overwhelm even the strongest social engineer. If the problem is to be solved, it must be done in little capsules. The problem is like an Alpean mountain, which seems immovable. It can only be removed if many millions of people decide to move it, one shovelful at a time.

I hereby present the problem, in its simplified form, and postulate a solution, which is do-able, a "shovelful" at a time. I also suggest that the problem must be tackled with a multi-pronged approach, dealing with all aspects of the problem: Socio-Cultural, Religious, Political, Economic, and Educational.

Section I

Historical Overview

Even though most Western history books trace the sojourn of Africans in America to the slave period, the historical truth is that Africans have been traveling to the so-called Americas for thousands of years. Ivan van Sertima documents artifacts which prove this, and which shows that pyramids of the type found in Africa have been found in the Americas—as well as boats and other evidence of the African presence.

There were also persons of African descent who traveled with Christopher Columbus on his voyages. One was captain of one of his three ships, but the most famous was Estevanico (Little Steven) who is credited with exploring the southeast and part of the southwest of what is now the United States of America.

The first African inhabitants of the colonies were domiciled in Jamestown, Virginia, in the year 1619, and they arrived with the first British colonists to the Americas. Later arrivals came in after the docking of the Mayflower, and they were classified as indentured servants. This was the status of most of the first few waves of slaves to arrive in the colonies. But let us pause a moment.

Let us look at slavery in the colonies, in perspective.

The passengers of the Mayflower were religious refugees and were interested in getting a safe haven from religious persecution. They were, therefore, self-sufficient and had no interest in exploring their new land for export and profit. (The shame is that they also participated in the annihilation of the Natives who were kind to them.) This could not be said, however, of the British and other European monarchies.

When the British crown established the colonies, they gave land grants to the elite aristocracy. These people were not inclined to migrate to the "wilderness" of these shores, so they hired agents to represent their interests. But land is worthless without production, so they had the dilemma of how to cultivate and what to plant. These were easily determined because the native Americans had helped the pilgrims to survive in the environment and showed them what to plant and how to do it.

The who to do it was resolved by the Crown, offering people in prisons and mental institutions release from their debts to society if they were willing to go to this new land, serve for seven years of indentured servitude, then be given freedom, as well as land of their own. Thousands accepted this offer and the initial workforce was put into place.

But they were not enough, so more workers had to be procured.

The Europeans had tried using the natives for manual, forced labor, but this proved to be unsuccessful because these people were not used to the prolonged, strenuous labor which was required to farm produce for export and profit. They were used to producing only what was required for their normal consumption. Furthermore, as was seen by the Spanish and Portuguese in the Caribbean, they would rather commit suicide than be enslaved by anyone. The only recourse was to "recruit" Africans for their labor.

The first "recruits" were offered the same deal as the European "servants" and, in fact, many hundreds of them were freed and given the land that was promised to them. There came a point, however, when some of the supervisors and land barons reasoned that it was expensive to pay for these people, and for their travel to the West. After all, they were different and should not be accorded the same humane treatment to which the Europeans had an entitlement.

So, the masters reasoned, the Africans could be kept in chattel slavery in perpetuity. After all, they asked, to whom would these Africans complain? And so the deed was done! Millions of men, women and children got caught up in the most cruel cycle of man's inhumanity to man, for over two hundred years. Furthermore, this condition of cruelty laid the framework for most inhuman interaction of the races in America to this very day.

Slavery was not endured without resistance. There was constant agitation against it on many different fronts. The fight was waged by slaves, as well as by "European" people of goodwill, all over the world.

In Jamaica, in the West Indies, the "maroons" put up such a fierce fight that, in order for the "institution" to survive, the British had to sign a treaty with Captain Cudjoe, Nanny, and others. In spite of the fact that the treaty called for the maroons to help capture and return other fugitive slaves to the British plantations, the still-enslaved Africans continued to fight so fiercely that slavery was abolished in Jamaica in 1834, effective in 1838 (see *Fight for Freedom).*

In Haiti, Toussaint L'Ouverture and his band succeeded in ousting the French and gaining manumission for the Haitians even before slavery was abolished in Jamaica and the British West Indies (see *The Haitian Maroons: Liberty or Death).* It is because of those victories by the slaves in Haiti and their embarrassment of the French that Haiti is still punished today by the European nations that salivate for its total demise.

Part of the success for the destruction of chattel slavery in the United States and the world has to be credited to the Englishman William Wilberforce and his colleagues in the anti-slavery movement in Britain. Their agitation caused the British government to ban the trans-Atlantic transport of slaves in any British vessel and British citizens from knowingly engaging in such activities. This decision effectively stymied the importation of slaves throughout the Americas.

Slavery was not dead, however, because an invention increased the effectiveness of cotton production and resuscitated the slave institution. Eli Whitney was erroneously given credit for this device, which made it profitable to process cotton and allowed the cotton gin to become the invention of the eighteenth century. So cotton was now king, but how was the planting of cotton going to be done to a degree which would make the gin's value be utilized? Easy! The slave-masters came up with a master plan. They created their own "hatchery."

Female slaves were designated as breeders and their jobs became one of producing children who were to fuel the continuation of slavery by adding new workers to the fold. Conversely, male slaves were designated as studs for the purpose of breeding the female slaves for the aforementioned purpose.

None of these slaves had a choice of who they slept with or to not sleep with anyone at all. And one can be sure that there were many of them who were not happy about the fact that they were breeding new babies to be trapped in the inhuman institution of slavery, in perpetuity. To those who may believe that the men had ideal situations, the answer is that there is no glory in being treated like a beast.

But the slaves, to a large degree, did not accept slavery without a fight. It is estimated that Africa lost more than fifty million souls to the trans-Atlantic slave trade, even though less than twenty million of those people actually arrived on these shores.

Many millions of Africans died fighting against capture on the continent. Many millions more died in the holding pens of Goree Island and other "transfer" areas. Add to that the many millions of casualties incurred in the holds of those devil ships, from which less than half the cargo emerged alive, and the human carnage was staggering, indeed. But it doesn't end there!

Hundreds of thousands of slaves were killed trying to escape slavery; thousands of others killed themselves and their families; many thousands of others were "lynched"; while others died trying to escape on the "underground railroad." The number of casualties is horrendous.

Slaves did a lot of different things to obtain their manumission. Many slaves worked hard, skimped and saved, and bought their freedom, as well of that of their families. But most slaves were not in that position, so they had to use other means.

So there were numerous uprisings! These included the Nat Turner "rebellion" where Turner, a slave preacher, was convinced that God had called him to save his people and so he organized a group of slaves to overthrow the slave-masters' regimes. He was, however, betrayed by some of his fellow slaves. After killing many slavers, he was captured and hanged.

Denmark Vesey fared no better. After similarly organizing his fellow chattel, he was also betrayed and punished. There were hundreds of other slave revolts which, though not succeeding in dislodging the slave-mongers were, nevertheless, successful in at least making them uncomfortable and fearful for their lives.

Other slaves did their parts, using different tactics. Harriet Tubman's strategy was to help organize the so-called "underground railroad." She returned to the South, time after time, to bring out dozens of slaves to freedom, notwithstanding the danger to her own life. Meanwhile, Sojourner Truth and Frederick Douglass, among others, were working with the anti-slavery movement to preach the anti-slavery doctrine throughout the north and to influence White people to lend their resources and their voices to the struggle. They succeeded in influencing people like William Garrison and his anti-slavery colleagues to wage a non-violent campaign as well as John Brown and his cohorts, who waged armed struggle and sacrificed their lives for the cause of freedom.

Dred Scott tried to use the legal system to obtain his freedom. Having accompanied his master to a "free" state, he believed, and argued, that he was free to walk away and not return to slavery. The courts ruled, however, that he was the property of his master, regardless of his geographical location.

The agitation of the anti-slavery operatives, the slave uprisings and the manumission of slaves in the British, French, Spanish and Portuguese territories—as well as the expansion of the U.S. to the west—caused a serious rift between the Southern slaveholders and the Northern states, resulting in a declaration of war between the States. In order to demoralize the South and "psychologically" recruit the "freed" slaves, President Lincoln decided to *"free"* the slaves in the rebel states.

Finally the Emancipation Proclamation was broadcast, the Civil War was fought, and the "freedom" was granted. But a new brand of bondage was instituted. A new chapter had begun. The chain was removed from the Africans' hands, but it was being tightened on their minds.

Furthermore, they were released without much social training or financial resources, so they remained at the mercy of the former slave-masters.

Booker T. Washington started a school to teach "negroes" self-sufficiency, and was labeled the leader of the freedmen, but he was not accepted by many of the newly-freed former slaves. His ideas were considered to be encouraging subservience. Enter William E. B. Du Bois, with his theory of the "talented tenth" and his ideas that the way to self-sufficiency was education. This was beyond the comprehension of most of those manumitted souls. So he was basically rejected.

Marcus Garvey then appeared, during the early twentieth century, to lead a large number of the masses. His back-to-Africa movement became very popular and he recruited many thousands of people, raised many millions of dollars, and actually relocated large numbers of people to Africa. Moreover, his movement was international and he actually started the Black Star Line, with a small fleet of ships for the repatriation mission.

He was, however, "brought down" by the U.S. government, with the aid of a bitter Du Bois, who was upset about being upended by the popularity of Garvey. The Garvey era gave way to the modern civil rights era of the 1950s and 1960s, with the rise to leadership and assassination of both Martin Luther King, Jr. and Malcolm X.

The civil rights era was one of the most turbulent times in the history of the United States, especially since it corresponded with the war, which was being waged in Vietnam. It was bad enough that the country was divided on the necessity and morality of the war, but the immorality of discrimination disgraced it in the eyes of the world. That exposure to world criticism, more than anything else, was responsible for the series of civil rights legislation and the weakening of the race-based interaction of Americans.

Busing became a major means of "integrating" communities but, as will be shown at a later time, that fiasco did not result in integrating the races. What it did was to cause a lot of fear and sleepless nights for hordes of helpless children, expose latent hate, and cause people to uproot themselves to avoid sharing their space with "those people." In the end, busing could not work because whenever the students were bused to a school, the residents of those school districts moved their children to other public schools, or to private schools. What happened next was that the best teachers were reassigned from the "integrated" schools to the less integrated schools in a school district.

Many Blacks who had been a part of the civil rights movement became co-opted by the system and, believing that they had made it, sometimes not only abandoned the fight for equal rights and justice, but became a hindrance to it. One such person (and there are many thousands) is a well-known Supreme Court Justice. There are also others who are mentioned elsewhere in this book, and each of us know many of these persons very well. Some even preach the abolition of affirmative action after they have benefited from it. After all, they will not be the "one monkey" if others are allowed the same opportunities!

Economics and electoral politics have elevated a few thousand African Americans to positions of influence and power, but for the overall population, things are still the same. A few Blacks have used the "quota" to take advantage of government and private contracts and to elevate themselves to economic independence but, overall, Blacks are much worse off economically than we were in the 1940s, 1950s, and 1960s. There are also many more Black elected officials and, although President Clinton had put some real power in the hands of Black cabinet-members, these officials were, for the most part, impotent.

The 1980s, under President Reagan, ushered in the "Age of Me-ism" when Americans became concerned about themselves to the exclusion of others, including family members, and so no valuable work was done toward bridging gaps, be they social, racial, or economic. Thankfully, the 1990s returned the country to the discussion of humanity and equity, led by President Clinton, who sponsored the discussion on racism in America.

Sad to say, the (s)election of George W. Bush returned the country to the "bushes", away from the stage of enlightenment, and to a drastic reversal of the few gains which the race had made.

History was, unexpectedly, made in 2008, with the election of the first African American president, Barack Obama. His election is being seen by many different people to mean many different things. While some people believe his election has catapulted us into the post-racial era, the opponents of racial peace and cooperation are "sharpening their bayonets" for an earnest resumption of battle.

President Obama has added only a sprinkling of black to the halls of power and the influence might not be significantly impacting.

It's "left to be seen" how it all plays out!

Section II

Social/Cultural Considerations

The September, 2001, attack on the World Trade Center and its aftermath have caused everyone to take pause and either consider or reconsider their place in the world, as well as the place of the world, and if and how it will survive. Everyone has been forced to look at race and racism, whether we like it or not because, although it seems that religion played the greatest role in that conflagration, the consequence of those aggressors' actions is that their race has played the greatest role. All Middle Easterners, as well as anyone who resembles that group in any way, have been targeted and condemned as "terrorists."

Not only has this occurrence opened up the nasty sores of racism and religious intolerance, but it has brought us all to the discussion of freedom. For those of us who only enjoyed true freedom in theory, it is a time to re-examine our plight in this world. For others, however, it is a time to think about what is freedom and what the price of that "freedom" might entail.

Post 9/11, there is a new Homeland Security Department, which monitors the movement of people and communication, with the result that there are severe restrictions on Americans, and others. This includes the installation of monitoring devices on the streets and in buildings, as well as wiretaps and other types of spying on citizens, which were heretofore "forbidden." The military and the CIA are also allowed to "interact" with American citizens at home.

The average American is now experiencing some of the "restrictions" which people of color have had to endure in this country over the hundreds of years. This is especially true of the experience of African Americans and Native Americans, as well as Hispanic Americans, to whom restrictions have increased many-fold. So the question is, what long-term impact will this have on the American psyche? It has to be concluded that if one gives up too much freedom for "security" then one will no longer live in the "land of the free."

But what difference does this make for the fourth-class citizen—the African American? Does the freedom and equality of the African American matter to the average American citizen? It would seem not, but that is not surprising based on the nature of man, and his inhumanity to others.

The noted philosopher, Thomas Hobbes, said that man was born in a "state of nature where there is a war of all against all." The only thing that saves us, he believes, is that we have formed societies, which not only protect us from outside forces, but also from ourselves.

Those who are unbelievers of this statement need only to look at the state of human nature and at history, especially as they relate to peoples of African ancestry throughout the world and the ages. The result of this war of all against all is the all-consuming racism one finds throughout the globe, especially in the United States of America.

America is the strongest world power (beginning in the middle of the twentieth century) and, as such, sets the tone for actions and behavior throughout the world. The practice of racism is no exception. For those who may protest this assertion, it is important to list a few examples.

Although Europeans, for the most part, have their reservations about interaction with African peoples and their share of racism, African people are treated with a lot more tolerance in Western Europe (Eastern Europe is more like America in its racism). Witness the fact that, over the years, many African Americans have had to move to Paris and other European destinations in order to get peace and recognition. African peoples are also allowed, on merit, to advance to greater heights in their careers in those venues. Further, witness the fact that soon after these "moderate" Europeans migrate to the United States they become some of the greatest proponents of separatism in this country. Some of them make the strongest claims to the bounty of the American dream for themselves and the withholding of these "morsels" from African Americans, whose forefathers, parents, and themselves built this country with their sweat, blood, and free labor.

Not by accident, the greatest amount of racist sentiment in Europe is found around American military bases because those natives who come into contact with the racists of the military adopt and adapt to their poisonous ways.

The foregoing is not to suggest that people in Europe are otherwise totally free of racism. They have practiced the subtle art for many centuries, and that is what caused them, at the Berlin Conference, in 1884-1885, to have the audacity to have believed they had the God-given right to sit and divide Africa amongst themselves. It is because of their racism that Haiti is so poverty-stricken today. It was not forgiven for breaking the chains of slavery and embarrassing Napoleon, nor for precipitating the destruction of the institution of slavery.

Had the inhabitants been white, they would have been lauded as great freedom fighters, *a la* the patriots of the American Revolution (who were not slaves, but fought only against oppressive taxation).

The U.S. is guilty of committing heinous crimes against its non-White population and exhibiting gross hypocrisy in the process. At the same time that the "patriots" were condemning the British crown for oppression and taxation without representation, while embracing the slogan, "Give me liberty or give me death," they held many thousands of Africans in chattel slavery. And they continued to do this for nearly two hundred years! Even after the slave has been "freed" he continues to be regarded as three-fifths of a man.

In all of its actions the United States continues to treat peoples and nations who are non-Europeans in a different way than it does to caucasians. As a matter of fact the U.S., as well as the other "European" countries, treat Spain and Portugal as somehow non-European, ostensibly because they are more mixed with the Moors who occupied southern Europe for hundreds of years. That fact may be responsible for Spanish-Americans and Portuguese-Americans being classified as Latino and treated as non-white even when their features are more caucasian than some northern Europeans.

Look at its stance, for example, on the so-called Middle East. On July 22, 1946, when the Jews bombed the King David Hotel in Jerusalem, murdering British citizens and Palestinians alike, they were not labeled as maniacal terrorists but they became respectable Israeli leaders who were embraced by the West. Why? They were European Jews. Are non-European Jews treated the same way, by America or by their Jewish brothers? The reports are that Falashas are not. One can understand that, after the holocaust, the Jews were desperate for a country of their own, so they did whatever they had to do to accomplish their goal. Palestinians feel they are in a holocaust situation.

Nor does America recognize the Palestinians (who occupied most of what is now Israel and who have been uprooted) as freedom fighters. Instead, they are labeled as "terrorists." Why?

I think that it is simply because they are non-Europeans. All other peoples of the Middle East are treated as inferior to the European Israelis. The result is that there will be no peace in the region. There is no unbiased arbitrator who can bring the parties together to legitimately discuss their issues. For those who believe the Bible, except for the Europeans who converted to Judaism, they are all descendants of Abraham, with an equal claim to the "covenant." I'm not taking sides because they worked well together in the African slave trade.

In another display of racism, the U.S. and Europe supported reparations for the European

Jews who were wronged by the Nazis and the Japanese who were wrongfully encamped during World War II, but what about the Native Americans and the African Americans? Americans refuse to entertain the idea of reparations to the people they robbed and held in slavery for those hundreds of years. This matter will be discussed in more detail in a later section.

The U.S. supported a regime in Cuba, which relegated its dark-skinned citizens to mostly menial labor, and boycotts one which preaches equality, ostensibly because it called Cuba a dictatorship, but it continued to support many dictators and communists throughout the world.

This is the backdrop from which we discuss the state of affairs in Black America.

The Dilemma

We will start with the dilemma faced by the slaves of the United States and their efforts to obtain freedom and continue the discourse to the point where we find ourselves today, followed by some possible solutions to the problems of our volunteer slavery.

The African Americans' struggle for freedom is an ongoing one. Following what may have been hundreds of "slave revolts," was the 1831 insurrection by Nat Turner. Nat Turner felt that he was chosen by the divine power to lead his people to freedom so, after an initial escape, he returned to his master in Southampton County, Virginia. Guided by what he thought a sign for action, he led a rebellion on August 21, which resulted in the death of about sixty Whites and more than one hundred slaves. He was captured on October 30, and executed, but his legacy was an encouragement to others who took similar types of action.

In speaking of the institution of slavery and the control of the slaves, the abolitionist Frederick Douglass made the following remarks:

> It was in the interest and business of slave holders to study human nature, and the slave nature in particular, with a view to practical results, and many of them attained astonishing proficiency in this direction. They had to deal not with earth, wood and stone, but with men, and by every regard they had for their own safety and prosperity they had need to know the material on which they were to work.
>
> Conscious of the injustice and wrong they were every hour perpetrating and knowing what they, themselves, would do were they the victims of such wrongs, they were constantly looking for the first signs of the dread retribution. They watched, therefore, with skilled and practical eyes, and learned to read, with great accuracy, the state of mind and heart of the slave, through his sable face. Unusual sobriety, apparent abstraction, sullenness, and indifference—indeed, any mood out of the

common way afforded ground for suspicion and inquiry.

In 1852, when Douglass was asked to speak at an "Independence" rally in Rochester, New York, he made the following response:

> I am not included within the pale of this glorious anniversary! Your high independence only reveals the immeasurable distance between us. The "blessings" in which you, this day, rejoice, are not enjoyed in common. The rich inheritance of justice, liberty, prosperity and independence bequeathed by your fathers, is shared by you, not by me. The sunlight that brought light and healing to you, has brought stripes and death to me. This Fourth of July is yours, not mine. You may rejoice; I must mourn. To drag a man in fetters into the grand illuminated temple of liberty, and call upon him to join you in joyous anthems, were inhuman mockery and sacrilegious irony. Do you mean, citizens, to mock me, by asking me to speak to-day? If so, there is a parallel to your conduct. And let me warn you that it is dangerous to copy the example of a nation whose crimes, towering up to heaven, were thrown down by the breath of the Almighty, burying that nation in irrevocable ruin! I can to-day take up the plaintive lament of a peeled and woe-smitten people!
>
> "By the rivers of Babylon, there we sat down. Yea! we wept when we remembered Zion. We hanged our harps upon the willows in the midst

thereof. For there, they that carried us away captive, required of us a song; and they who wasted us required of us mirth, saying, Sing us one of the songs of Zion. How can we sing the Lord's song in a strange land? If I forget thee, O Jerusalem, let my right hand forget her cunning. If I do not remember thee, let my tongue cleave to the roof of my mouth."

The problems of the African American have been long-standing and severe. Throughout the years a large number of writers, Black and White, have addressed them from many varied perspectives. For example, in his 1908 book, *Following the Color Line,* Ray Stannard Baker deals with "American Negro citizenship in the progressive era."

He begins, in describing the Atlanta riot of 1906:

> Upon the wave of antagonism between the white and Negro races in this country, there arises occasionally a wave, stormy in its appearance, but soon subsiding into quietude.... That spectacular though superficial disturbance, the disaster incident and the remarkable efforts at reconstruction will lead the way naturally—as human nature is best interpreted in moments of passion—to a clearer understanding of the deep and complex race feeling which exists in this country.

The author investigated the race question by region and exclaimed surprise at how much time is consumed—by both Black and White—discussing the problems of race. For example, he mentions the case of a Black boy who had obtained a position as a butler's assistant in a prominent White household. When he was asked by his family and cohorts what were the subjects of discussion in the household, he replied, "Mostly they discusses us cullud folks."

Although he states that Northerners were not so preoccupied with the subject, he concedes that it was also an important topic of discussion.

In his 1933 book, *The Miseducation of the Negro,* Carter G. Woodson discusses, at length, the plight of the Negro in America. In his chapter on "How We Missed the Mark," Woodson states:

> How we have arrived at the present state of affairs can be understood only by studying the forces effective in the development of Negro education since it was systematically undertaken immediately after Emancipation. To point out merely the defects as they appear today will be of little benefit to the present and future generations. These things must be viewed in their historic setting. The conditions of today have been determined by what has taken place in the past, and in a careful study of this history we may see more clearly the great theatre of events in which the Negro has played a part. We may understand better what his role has been and how well he has functioned in it.

With regard to training, he suggests that the schools, which were set up, were so inadequate that even those Negroes who did make some effort to learn, did not actually receive either the industrial or the classical education. In fact, those with industrial training were taught to master techniques that were already discarded in progressive centers. Likewise, he postulated, the classical training produced few thinkers and philosophers. He added that "even men like Roland Hayes and Henry O. Tanner have risen to the higher levels by getting out of this country to relieve selves of our stifling traditions and to recover from their education."

The Race Factor

With regard to racial tolerance, things have not become much different, in 2010, than they were in 1831 and before. In the mid-1990s a White Congressman received over 500 pieces of hate mail, along with over 150 phone calls of like stripe, for having the nerve to suggest that the Congress of the United States should apologize to African Americans for slavery. One Texan went as far as to suggest that the U.S. government owed him and his family "$135 million for slaves his great-great grandfather lost at the end of the Civil War."

On July 28, 1997, Rev. Joseph Lowery, retiring head of the Southern Christian Leadership Conference, and a former colleague of the Rev. Dr. Martin Luther King, Jr., acknowledged that some progress had been made during the 1960s, with respect to civil rights. He was, however, quick to add that the government has eroded these gains over the years. According to him, they have totally destroyed affirmative action. He said, "Too much tears have been shed, too many people have died, too much sweat has been used . . . for us to allow this destruction of our rights to take place."

Rev. Lowery was being honored for his years of untiring efforts on behalf of the emancipation of his people, by the organization that had the leadership role in organizing and mobilizing the "soldiers" for liberty, which had been led by Dr. King.

One can only imagine how Dr. Lowery felt, watching his life's work disintegrate before his eyes. After all, he had placed his life, and that of his family, on the line for the struggle. If one can feel such sad disappointments for minor everyday setbacks, then this erosion of the small human rights gains must be devastating, indeed. The fact that he was being recognized by many dozens of dignitaries, Black and White, might have taken some of the sting from his "wounds" and, hopefully, encouraged him in the fact that there have been many converts and some will remain strong in the struggle. Hopefully, those converts will proselytize and continue the conversions.

In a classic case of the devil quoting scripture to support her wrongdoing, the news media, next day featured a White man who acknowledged that racism does exist in America, "especially in Atlanta, where only Black mayors are elected." He added that there are many qualified Whites who don't have a chance of becoming mayor.

This author has thought long and hard, but can't think of hearing about or reading of a single incident in these many hundreds of years of White rule when a White person said that there were many qualified Blacks who deserve the chance to be elected to office. What about the governorship of Georgia? What about just removing the Confederate symbol from the Georgia and South Carolina state flags because it's a distressing reminder to African Americans of slavery and Jim Crow?

He gave the impression that Black people vote only for people of our own kind. That is the farthest thing from the truth because nine hundred and ninety-nine of every one thousand candidates is white and we vote for, or against, them all the time. So why should we be vilified when we vote for someone who looks like us? Racists be damned!

It is true that racism may not be as entrenched in some areas as it used to be. Predominantly White constituents have elected mayors in Denver,

Seattle and Cleveland, etc, as well as a governors in Virginia and Massachusetts and, now a president of the United States. That is how it should be, and people should be chosen on their merits. However, we are a long way off from the time when that will happen as a matter of course. Until then, we just have to do for self, and continue to prove our worth.

Racism is also entrenched in our psyche. There are writers and analysts, politicians and social workers, and educators and "civil rights" advocates, ethicists and scholars, and ordinary citizens of a dark hue who are so filled with self-hatred that they have continued the charge to depreciate the value of the African in America and the world.

We are not speaking of people outside of our community, but of people who are reluctant members. These people run the gamut of socio-economic giants to paupers. They range from those who would wish to change their skin to those who wish to disassociate with it, altogether. There are, also, those people who stop at nothing to disassociate themselves from the community, even when their skin is dark. Note the following example:

In a news program *(48 Hours?)* aired the third week of November, 2003, a Louisiana school principal told the story of his DNA test results.

It seems that this gentleman, being a "proud" African American, had "taught" his two children about his African heritage as well as African pride. His "curiosity," however, got the best of him, so he was driven to obtain his DNA profile. He paid his approximately $600.00 and anxiously awaited the result. Finally, it came.

The exact breakdown of his profile is not the important thing. The greater percentage of his profile showed him to be Native American and Euro-Indian. He supposedly had a "zero" percentage of African DNA, according to the profile. He, triumphantly, proclaimed that on his next census report he would register as a Native American.

This story is important because it exposes a malady, which is pervasive in our society and our community. First of all, the stigma attached to being Black is alive and well not only in the Black community but, seemingly, in all communities. The gentleman in question is black in complexion and reported being called "nigger" on many occasions. He will continue to be called that, notwithstanding his new Native American moniker.

Secondly, although he expressed his African pride and his nurturing of his children in that vein, he had divorced his Black wife and married a white woman. His partly-black children, notably, have non-black partners. So it seems that the pride had not stuck in any of them (or it had dissipated).

The indications of this case are that this gentleman looked at his curly hair, at his mother (who seemed to be a mulatto), and at other family members, and set out to prove that he is not African American.

Having read somewhere that the DNA of everyone whom one kisses remains in one's mouth forever and, considering that this man is married to a caucasian woman, this writer's question is, how much of *her* DNA was swabbed and is calculated with his and, by extension, how accurate can the DNA test be, in that case?

The above case highlights a trend that is now prevalent in the United States—the movement away from classifying races into the three basic groups: caucasoid, mongoloid, or negroid. This has come about as people of mixed races (especially those including negroid) no longer want to be denigrated by being called Negro, and as others, especially politicians, have sought to use this mechanism as a "divide and conquer" tool. Be that as it may, many of those "others" welcome the opportunity to be "better" than their "neighbors" who are African Americans.

There are Negroes who are angry at their negritude and are avid proponents of eliminating any idea of assistance for people of color. They are the oppressors' best friends. Some of them are paid, handsomely, for their advocacy of the elimination of such organizations as the NAACP and the SCLC, amongst others, while others are angry that they are not white, so they want to destroy anyone and anything which remind them of their blackness and, therefore, their "inferiority."

Elsewhere in this book I refer to those people who are working against our interest and suggest how they should be handled. I make allowance for those who think that they are doing the right thing. For example, there are politicians who "sell out" the community in an effort to serve their own narrow constituency. They are wrong in their actions because, in the long run, what is good for the whole community is what counts. Not what is beneficial to a few! So, although we can condemn them for "selling" out, it is their ignorance that should be indicted rather than their motive.

Some others betray us in their greed for power and riches. Those should be condemned and ostracized. But it is those people who are utterly stupid and suffer from an inferiority complex; those who glorify the European to the extent that they sell the rest of us to the highest bidder, who are to be banished, posthaste, by whatever means necessary. They are the cancer that is strangling the Black community and causing us not to grow. They are the ones mis-educating our children and helping to send them to the streets, the prisons, and the grave. They are the ones who are telling us that we are no good and that the White man is good to us in releasing us from slavery and providing us with welfare, because we cannot handle workfare.

Neighborhoods

The neighborhoods in which African Americans live are almost always inferior to that in which White people reside. As a matter of fact, many Black folks clamor to live in "White" neighborhoods, for a variety of reasons:

1. They have a feeling that they have "made it" if they can afford to live amongst these other folks.

2. They feel more secure in those neighborhoods because there is better protection and better service.

3. The neighborhood is "better kept" and there is not the stigma of living in a "slum."

4. The children will have better schools and mix with a higher class of schoolmates, etc.

5. They feel more kinship to White folks, especially if they blame other Blacks for their lot. These are people who feel that Whites have done no harm to Blacks, have allowed us all the opportunities, and that we are the ones who lack ambition and, therefore, cause our own miseries. There are many examples of these kinds of Blacks, and some are mentioned here.

While, some of these considerations seem valid, there are negative sides to all of them.

With respect to "making it", the best scenario would be for those successful people to remain in their communities, help to build them and be role models to children and adults, alike. Their sojourn in the community would accrue benefits to the community.

Secondly, the "security" which some see for themselves in the White community is generally a false one. The first reaction of most Whites, when a person of color moves into their neighborhood, is to run from that area. There seems, however, to now be a trend in New York City, and elsewhere, for the children of those who fled their old neighborhoods to return, pricing the present inhabitants out of their homes.

The security issue is also overrated because there have been thousands of incidents where Blacks and other "minority" groups have been targeted, injured and killed for having the audacity to move into white neighborhoods, while the authorities either turn a blind eye, or participate in the acts.

To our disgrace, other neighborhoods are better kept than ours are, even though we are sometimes the ones who help keep those other neighborhoods clean. We feel that we do not have ownership of the houses in which we live, so we have no obligation to keep them clean and in good repair. We think that we have no right to ask (or demand) that our neighbors do their part to maintain the beauty of our buildings and landscape. We abhor the scarring of the buildings with graffiti, but we would rather move than fight for the integrity of our neighborhoods. We have to remember that it may be the man's house, but it is our home, so it is up to us to keep it clean and tidy. Furthermore, we should always have the thought that ours is a temporary stay on someone else's property, because the goal should always be ownership.

We seek better schools and a higher class of schoolmates for our children and that is to be applauded, but we put our children in extremely stressful positions. We often place them in environments where they are not wanted by students, or by teachers, and these people often vent their venom on these poor, innocent souls. We need to consider that the nurturing environments with teachers and students like themselves are more beneficial and calming. That is not to say that there aren't some people in the alien environment who will welcome and nurture our children, but they are few and far between.

Our neighborhoods are filled with old buildings that, through being built with toxic materials, coupled with years of neglect, have become deathtraps to our community, filled with poison and danger. They are inhabited with rats, roaches, and other vermin which spread diseases from one wretched occupant to another and wreaks havoc on the community.

The result is that the healthcare needs are multiplied, while the support system is diminished. This state of affairs causes a situation in the Black community where the rate of illness is significantly enhanced versus that in other communities. The life-span of the average Black is more than eight years less than that of the White, with the quality of life (ill-health, frustration) being much worse.

Blacks have a much higher onset of diseases such as AIDS, diabetes, tuberculosis, asthma, high blood pressure, and other related diseases than their counterparts. Surprisingly, we have less mental illness.

Many conscious individuals and organizations have organized health seminars in order to screen and treat both mental and physical illnesses, and they should be applauded. We need to organize many more of these types of outreach, however, because only a small fraction of our community is being served by those active participants.

We are not able to benefit from preventive care, as do most other people, because of lack of health insurance coverage. The 2009-2010 "debate" over health care coverage illuminated the selfishness of most Americans, who do not care one iota for the interest of others (Black or White) as long as they themselves are "protected."

Because most Black persons live in poverty, they are prone to all the ills of poverty. Some of these ills are crime, police brutality or neglect, drug use and abuse, prostitution, family abuse, and the like.

If one is poor and therefore wields no influence, the authorities neglect to give the services that others get. Police protection is one such service. As we see in innumerable instances, police abuse is what we get, instead. Witness the shooting of Amadou Diallo, the brutalization of Rodney King, Abner Louima, and the murder and maiming of thousands of Blacks by the police who are sworn to protect, and we see the different levels of protection afforded our community, and others.

Even Black police are in jeopardy from their "colleagues." They are either deliberately killed by conspiracy or from "friendly fire."

Crime is rampant in our backyards and no one seems to be willing to protect us from it. As a matter of fact, there seems to be an attitude that crime will exist, anyway, so it should be cordoned off within the Black community so as to protect the other neighborhoods from it. Note how many times other people come to the black neighborhood to buy drugs, play the numbers, buy prostitutes, and the like. Compare that with the numbers of known cases where Blacks are picked up in White neighborhoods and we find it almost nonexistent.

Drug and alcohol abuse is usually more pronounced amongst those who have the least hope for a bright future and so, it is not surprising that the incident of abuse is extremely high in our community. People try to drown their sorrows by flying off to a psychedelic, unreal world, leaving the troubles behind.

By far the most devastating effect of poverty is the number of homeless and un-adopted children in the Black community. Many of them are orphaned by their dead AIDS parents; removed from families because of abuse or neglect; given up by teenage mothers who are unable to care for them; or removed from drug-addicted parents or just abandoned. The result is that they flounder in institutions or foster homes for years, exposed to ill influences, having no hope, and ending up being part of the new cycle of hopelessness and despair. They need to be saved!

Therefore, we must team up with our community organizations and our individual citizens, family and friends (in other words, the "village") in order to save our children. We have strayed from the village concept in which all the parents are responsible for all the children, and we have gone to the failed idea of the nuclear family. That concept hasn't ever worked and will never work. It's truly nurturing families, especially the Black family, which has always needed the extended tentacles of individual members for its survival.

Solutions

Once upon a time, the people in the Black community were conscious of the fact that it takes a whole village to raise a child. It also took a whole village to protect a single resident. We have strayed from the idea that we are our brothers' keepers, with the result that no one is our keeper. We are, therefore, exposed to the whims of every other group and so we remain the whipping boy of every other community. We need to recognize our plight, rise up and make ourselves right. We must adhere to the following rules and pull ourselves out of the doldrums.

We must empower ourselves by joining, and supporting organizations (there are many) which work for the betterment of the community. Our involvement strengthens the organizations both in terms of their manpower and their leverage in securing funds and influence to better serve us.

We need to become neighborhood "watchers" in order to reduce the proliferation of drugs, as well as other crimes in our community. By being involved, we serve notice on the police and other authorities that they have to both protect us from the criminals and from their own abuse. We also serve notice on the criminals that they cannot and will not get away with committing crimes in our neighborhoods. Our vigilance will encourage investments in our communities, which will further enhance the value of property and provide a better quality of life.

We need to monitor the actions of all who interact within the community and get involved in boycotts, demonstrations, and other civil actions, as necessary, in order to alert whomsoever necessary, that we mean business and will not tolerate other than positive input into our community.

We need to contribute, financially or otherwise, to the organizations that protect, or fight to protect, human rights. These organizations must be supported and strengthened because they are vital in supporting our rights as human beings. This is especially critical at a time such as this when all vestiges of human rights seem to be eroding all over the globe.

We must continue to monitor the actions of the police and other parties who are supposed to protect our community to make sure that our interests are advanced. We must protect the innocent from the brutality of inhumane operatives.

On September 28, 2003, Ed Bradley reported a story of blood-curdling proportions about a racist undercover detective in Tulia, Texas, who managed to get half of the Black population convicted and sent to prison by a White jury on drug charges and prostitution. It did not matter that this policeman was, himself, a convicted felon with no legitimate standing as either a citizen or a lawman. Luckily, some good souls realized the injustice and intervened to get the charges thrown out, and the victims released.

We must support building of schools and community-support organizations and stop the proliferation of the building of prisons, courthouses and half-way houses for our children. We must educate our youth concerning what to do when confronted by the police or any other "authority" figures, so that they are not entrapped or framed, with the resulting destruction of their "successful" future.

We must encourage investments in the community, both in economic and human resources. Too many times we find that the successful people from the community move away and invest in other people's communities, while neglecting their "roots." The community can only grow and progress with the help of the "brains" and "brawn" of those successful members.

With regard to health issues, we need to organize many more seminars on healthy living and agitate to have health care opportunities within the community. It does not matter how aware we become of the need for health care and healthy living if we do not access the diagnostic and treatment resources.

Our children are our greatest resources and our hope for the future of the race, yet we allow them to be cast aside and led astray. Granted that the role of parenting rests upon the shoulders of people who either don't know how to parent (because of the "nuclear family" mentality and the drifting away from the council of the older folks, or because the parents just don't know what to do and just won't ask). However, parenting is the role of everyone in the community.

A middle-aged black gentleman recently commented that one of the problems with the community is that many teenagers, especially male, dare the elders of the community to "meddle into their affairs." He was right in his observation and we should take it seriously, but we face a dilemma. The fact is that if we want to preserve the community we have an obligation to meddle. That is not to suggest that all of us should meddle in each person's affairs, but we should at least be our brothers' and sisters' keepers. The challenge is to establish and maintain dialogue with our people—especially the children—in spite of their resistance.

With the thought of the global village as our guiding light, all of us should seek to adopt or otherwise care for those children who are orphans or who are abandoned. Given a chance at a good life they might become significant contributors to the development of our community and the world.

We need to begin, today, to excise the malady of "divide and conquer" which has caused so much discord in our community. It is a tool that is used, overtly and covertly, by the oppressors of our people. We are divided along many lines: Africans v. African Americans; West Indians v. African Americans; West Indians v. Africans; Jamaicans v. Trinidadians; Guyanese v. Barbadians; New Yorkers v. Georgians; Northerners v. Southerners; Brooklynites v. Manhattanites, etc.

We are divided based on our hue: who is dark chocolate, light chocolate; dark, light, or damned near white; our hair texture; and our neighborhoods. We are divided by politics, religion, social circles, and by anything we can conjure up, so that we constantly work toward our own failure and desolation.

Only when we begin to unite all the aspects of our community will we begin to make progress. Among other things, we need to recognize and utilize the following organizations within our community (as well as others) in addition to creating other functional organizations.

Fraternities & Sororities

Fraternities and sororities abound in the Black community and most of them are doing significant work, which goes unnoticed by the majority of people.

These organizations feed the hungry and take care of the homeless; they provide recreational and educational assistance to children; they give scholarships and guidance to needy students; they connect the readership with authors to promote literacy and reading; they sponsor field trips to colleges and many historical sites; they build homes, fight for civil rights, and they do a myriad of other significant things.

Sororities and fraternities provide support and guidance to students and to each other, while encouraging excellence and teamwork.

The only shortcoming is that some of these organizations spend too much time competing with one another instead of coalescing on certain projects, thus avoiding duplication and wasted efforts.

The importance of their existence and their work seem not to be recognized by the average person, but if one of these organizations was to adopt a project and run with it, that project would be almost guaranteed success.

Freemasons

We are not sure whether freemasons become successful people or successful people become freemasons, but most freemasons seem to be successful in their chosen endeavors.

Although their goings-on are secret, their "codes" introduce them to one another, and they "open doors" for each other. If they were to "organize" to fully extend their help to the community on a sustained, cooperative basis, the community would be greatly benefited.

"Social" Clubs

Social clubs include *Sports Clubs, Travel Clubs, Reading Clubs,* and the like, and they cater to the well-being of their members.

Social clubs generally provide a respite from the everyday drudgery of life but, on a wider scale, they can also act as catalysts for the enhancement of the quality of life in the African American community.

It is a gospel that it is the people who most need recreation who usually lack the ability to enjoy it. These clubs, therefore, provide such needed distractions and should be much more popular than they are.

Social clubs, of course, include those organizations that have dances and parties solely for the enjoyment of their patrons and the financial enrichment of their sponsors. These are not the ones being lauded.

The clubs being praised are the ones that are formed basically to enhance the interaction and enjoyment of their patrons, while at the same time increasing their awareness of, and commitment to, the betterment of their social-cultural experience. Social clubs contribute to the strengthening of and as a support to many immigrant groups in different parts of the world and have been significant in their role as beacons to help navigate these new peoples through the rough "waters" in their new lands.

There are also other social clubs, but they are mostly used to shuttle boys and girls into "society" or to be the bourgeoisie platform for certain elite "blue-veiners" from which to spout their "superiority" and aloofness.

Social clubs can be used to educate and to elevate people of color. Instead of some of them being used to sprout and spout pomposity, they can be used as tools of inclusion and consciousness-raising. They can be used to deprogram youths who are going to be some of the leaders in our community and to reprogram them to the fact of the importance of Africans in history and our importance in the future of the world.

Investment Clubs can sometimes be considered as quasi-social clubs, in that they are groups which support the psychological need for friendship and camaraderie between its members, while trying to fill their bank accounts with the profit from their investments. One of the main problems in our community is that we don't understand the value and use of money. Maybe the reason is that we have not been able to retain enough to be comfortable with it. We are always chasing it and it always seems to be eluding us. Investment club members need to reach out to community youth and teach them the dynamics of proper money management and use.

Boys' & Girls' Clubs

The Boys' and Girls' Scouts and the Boys' and Girls' Clubs of America are social clubs designed to work for the involvement and training of boys and girls. They can be useful tools for teaching tolerance and brotherhood, but that is not the focus of the leaders. However, if such organizations abide by their credos, then they should teach that in order to have better people and a better world, tolerance of normal human social behavior, and brotherhood should be part of the training.

Kiwanis, Lions, Rotary, Key Clubs, etc.

These clubs are "membered" by people who are socially conscious and who also have a yen for socialization. Kiwanians, and others, have members in almost every city in the western world, with worldwide connections and a level of goodwill with one another. These sorts of connections allow for people of goodwill to exchange ideas for raising funds and giving charity to people who are in need. While recognizing the good work that they do, more benefits can be ascertained if they recognize their need to refocus their efforts to helping people who are needy to get the “leg-up” to launch them on the road to success. These relationships can then be exploited for the greater good of the community and the world.

We need to learn how to properly use our organizations for our enlightenment and upliftment instead of for competition because only by doing so can we obtain the substantial benefits that can be accrued by these organizations.

Section III

Religious Involvement

And it came to pass that, in the age of enlightenment, religion became the guidepost for racism, slavery, and man's inhumanity to man. There became a time when Popes endorsed slavery of human beings in the "New World".... When ministers preached the goodness and the worthiness of chattel servitude in erasing the "curse of Ham". ...When the "religious" forefathers of the American colonies intoned "give me liberty or give me death" in response to "taxation without representation" while "valuating" the Negro as three-fifths human.... When a "born-again Christian" president, while governor, advocated the death penalty for a retarded person while condemning a woman's right to choose (and family planning) and claiming moral suasion as he unilaterally declared war on a people and murdered tens of thousands of innocent men, women and children. It did not even matter to him that thousands of Americans were killed in the battles and millions more were put at risk. "Collateral Damage", he called it.

Religion has always been misused and abused, and it has always been a tool used by demagogues to justify their horrendous actions. These people have always invoked God and claimed that “He” was on their side. God has always been presented as “just”. If God is just, then what side does “He” take if all parties claim to be doing “His” work?

Religion has evolved to the point that this author is afraid of people who claim to be religious because they seem to perpetrate much more evil than those who claim to be less than good, or those who make no claim at all.

Religion is supposed to be the most powerful force for good, since it is, by its very nature, a communication tool with the Almighty Force(s) of nature at “Its” very best and most merciful.

However, as practiced by all religious entities, religion has become the most destructive human-“controlled” force in the world. Consider this: more people have been enslaved, killed, framed and otherwise disenfranchised in the name of religion than for any other cause. The influence of sex is a far second.

One has only to examine the Bible to see the historical “beginnings” of holy wars and to see how devastating those conflicts were. In most cases the claims were that God had instructed His people to wipe out offending nations.

During the “Dark Ages” in Europe, there was the 700-Year War, which the Catholic Church waged against the “Infidels.” These Infidels happen to have been the Moors, who had invaded Europe through North Africa, bringing their Moslem religion into Europe. This was not only a religious, but also a race war, since the Moors were mostly Black Africans. The fact that is mostly ignored is that these Moors brought enlightenment to Europe, pulling it out of the Dark Ages and advancing it through the Middle Ages to its "Renaissance" period (see *The Rape of Paradise).*

We continued to see religious upheavals and catastrophes in Europe and the rise of Martin Luther, with his Protestant ethic and the break of large numbers of people from the Catholic Church. This culminated in many thousands of religious refugees migrating to the American colony on the *Mayflower* and other ships.

With the advent of the scourge of chattel slavery, the Southern church was front and center in the justification of the theory of the "curse of Ham." It was the church which told the slaves (a religious people) that the slave-masters' God had promised that if the Africans were good slaves, they would be rewarded, when they died, by going to heaven (the Black side?).

From the mid-twentieth into the twenty-first century, the main religious contention (and source of many thousands of murders) has been the Israeli "homeland" vs. the Palestinian "homeland." Translated, it is the war of the Jews against the Arabs.

This situation has now escalated into a major conflict that threatens to culminate into World War III, with "Fundamentalist Christians" supporting Israel and encouraging escalation of the conflict (which they see as prophecy) to speed up armageddon. On the other hand, Arabs are escalating their attacks on the "non-Arab" peoples and pushing the world further to the brink of catastrophe.

Having dealt with the problem of religion in this world, let me get a little more specific and deal with some of the negatives of religion in the United States.

Based on the actions of "Christians" in the U.S., especially the Fundamentalists, if Christ had lived today, and preached the message which he had, he would have been branded an heretic and crucified by them. Their dogma and practice are so un-Christian that they bear no resemblance to Christ.

Imagine calling people like former Attorney General Ashcroft and President George W. Bush "born-again" Christians? What is Christian about them? How are they Christ-like?

They are both racist (maybe they are only anti-African!); both act in the interest of the rich and discriminate against the poor; they are both mean-spirited; they both fail to forgive their "brother" even once, not to mention seventy times seven; and they are both unyielding, whether they are right or wrong, among other un-Christian traits.

It is the “born-again Christian” G.W. Bush who, as Governor of Texas, refused to stay the execution of a retarded man on death row. After he was murdered, he was shown to be innocent. These “gentlemen” are just two Southern Christians who proudly brand themselves as Conservatives.

I have news for these people. Jesus was a Liberal! Jesus said, among other things, “Love thy neighbor as thyself.” This was a confirmation of the edict in the “Ten Commandments.” He practiced this by interacting with the Gentiles, going to their weddings and otherwise communing with them. Some of his best friends were Gentiles.

Jesus said, “Forgive your brother seventy times seven...” but these new-day Christians say, “Onward Christian soldiers, marching on to war, to kill the dirty bastards....” The so-called Christians fly the Confederate flag, even though it is a reminder of the civil War, it is divisive to the nation, and is salt in the sore of African Americans as a reminder of the days of chattel slavery.

These “Christians” are “pro-life”, yet they kill “pro-choice” advocates when they blow up family planning and abortion clinics. What is more, they do not hesitate to kill people who are accused of committing crimes. They are the most prolific war-mongers and they carry the “biggest” sticks to beat all non-Americans “who don’t submit to the American will and those Americans who oppose any of their programs or actions." Whereas Christ said, "Give unto Caesar what is Caesar's and unto God what is God's" these people want to merge God with Caesar, and oppose separation of church and state. Furthermore, they have no aversion to disenfranchising anyone who is not a "Christian" (or Jew).

They claim support Israel in the Palestinian situation, only because they want a showdown in that region to hasten armageddon and fulfill prophecy. The conclusion is they don't understand Christ or that they are anti-Christ (*The Bible*, 1 John 2).

These Fundamentalists pride themselves on dividing America into Red and Blue states, unconcerned with the implications of a divided America. They based their voting (especially in the 2004 and 2008 Presidential elections) on "moral values," including the heretofore mentioned right-to-life and anti-homosexuality, but there are many, more critical issues that they totally ignored.

While most reasonable persons who are not homosexuals do not overtly support the lifestyle, the selection of a president who is not sensitive to the needs of most of the nation (senior citizens, the infirmed, the poor, and the children, etc.), who mortgages our grandchildren's lives and who doesn't understand the world and so gets us into a war we cannot win, is ludicrous and stupid. All of our citizens must feel that their voices will be and are being heard.

While lambasting the Fundamentalists, we must not forget the other religionists who, although maybe less egregious, have abdicated their roles in making this world a better place. They are the Catholic priests who are abusing children, others passing amendments to admit sexual offenders to the priesthood (even though these offenders are abusing children), while still others are using religion for their own economic and political gains or to further one hate-festering cause or another. Instead of preaching brotherhood, they are fostering interdenominational competition and skepticism at the very least, and hatred at its worst.

The Black church, which we Black folk are expecting to be our beacon, is equally filled with rogues, whoremongers, and preachers and deacons stealing in the name of the Lord.

The preachers boast of their excessive wealth while their members take their own rent and food money to support them because "our pastors must go in style." It does not matter to that they are admonished to "tend to the flock" and to "seek and save those who are lost." Their prerogative is to seek and to save all the dollar bills that might slip from their fingers.

The Christian must attempt to be Christ-like and to "love one another" as Christ asked. And Christians are not the only people convicted by their faith to show love and compassion. Those are the tenets of all religions and, if practiced by the "believers," there would be peace on earth.

This author believes that part of the problem with the church is that the members, and leaders, alike, excuse their behavior by invoking the "Jesus was the only man without sin" argument. One "elder" said that once one becomes a Christian all of one's sins will be forgiven. He rejected the argument that a Christian is a "recovering sinner," like members of A.A. are recovering alcoholics. In other words, one has to work, constantly, to avoid sin and to do good. One will "fall off the wagon" and sin, sometimes, but he/she is always conscious and striving to do good. It does not mean consciously hurting, harming, and doing "sinful" things to others, believing these sins are automatically forgiven because one calls oneself a Christian.

The foregoing malady is not exclusive to Protestant Christians, or to one denomination of that faith. I've had Catholic "religious" friends who did less than good things during the week, went to confession on Saturday, to church on Sunday, and went back to the same deeds on Sunday afternoon. The Jewish "practitioners", probably in most instances, do the same things all year, pray for forgiveness on the "day of atonement", and continue with their normal actions the next day. The Muslims have their Ramadan and, just as happens with other religions, they revert to their less than religions actions the day the celebration is over. The other "religious" persons of the world are likewise guilty of hypocrisy, and that is why we are still struggling to find peace and equality.

The fact is that man is inhumane to man, but they all hide behind the institutions of religion and pretend to be good. They have given goodness a bad name, and they lie and steal in the name of "God."

That is the nature of religion in our time and, since religion is the instigator and barometer of goodness and justice, it is no wonder that the world is full of evil and inhumanity. Thus, the dilemmas of racism, religious intolerance and perversion threaten to strangle us all.

It is no wonder that "God" allows the churches to be burned!

In a 1957 interview, the "great" crusader, Rev. Billy Graham, was asked why, at the time of a seeming increase in church attendance and conversions, the crime rate—as well as racial intolerance—seemed to be on the rise. His reply was that while people publicly acknowledged these problems, they did not practice at home the principles of Christianity, which would help to eradicate these problems. He was part of the problem. He did not insist to his segregated audiences that there was to be no separation of "God's people." He did not expel the overt racists but continued to tiptoe around the abomination of their actions. He also sins who closes his eyes to injustice.

Forty-plus years later, Rev. Graham continued to preach the gospel of "brotherhood in Christ" and the "Christians" continued to commit crimes and practice racism. His son is worse, thinking he had a "right" to be invited to the white house because he's a "well-known" minister. Pope John Paul II admonished Catholics to practice brotherhood and tolerance, as do many other religious leaders but hatred is rising at an alarming rate. Many religious leaders preach brotherhood, but do not practice it.

Take the example of doctrine. Each religion and each denomination preaches that its belief is the correct one and that all others are flawed. Each suggests that the "faithful" cling to one another and avoid the company of "evil-doers."

They do not conclude that each can reap "the kingdom of God" if he or she lives by conscience, based on an individual interpretation of biblical (or Torah, Koran, Pali Papers, etc.) teachings.

Starting with intolerance for other religions, the "church" sows the seed of discord that permeates each community and each country.

How can any religious leader who portends to teach tolerance accept even one intolerant parishioner? The fact is that in many religious orders prejudice goes hand-in-hand with dogma. Some religions even teach that they are "God's chosen people" and treat everyone else as though they are repulsive and unworthy of consideration. They interact with other people only to the extent that they themselves benefit from the relationship.

If one looks at religious interaction, one will realize that more evil has been perpetrated in the name of religion than for any other cause. The aforementioned 700-year war, in Europe, reported as the Catholic Church's "war against the infidels" was a race war, with White Europeans fighting to expel the African Moors from Europe. The conflict, which lasted in Ireland for dozens of years, was a religious war. The present-day Israeli-Arab war is a religious war with severe racial overtones. Prior to, and in-between these wars are thousands of religious/racial conflicts with unbelievable carnage.

The wars continue today and take on many forms. One is the destruction of houses of worship, as well as religious symbols and artifacts. Because of the important role the Black church has played in the liberation of African Americans, it has become a favorite target. One popular method for its destruction has been burning.

So They Burn the Churches!

They burn the churches, and by so doing, they have launched an attack on the very heart of the African American community.

Example after example is presented to us in the media to suggest that the burnings are not accidents or acts of God.

And what is being done? There are mild protests from a very few quarters and the "sinners" are, for the most part, left to the wrath of God. But, as most of us know very well, God helps those who help themselves.

It is the Bible that admonishes believers to don the armor of God and to defend His holy places. The only conclusion this author can reach is that all who claim to be religious should protect their religion, with their lives, if necessary. But the African-American community has been used to its holy places being desecrated. Only a few years ago, the former Mayor of the City of New York, Giuliani, defended the rights of his police to raid a mosque in the Village of Harlem. Not long before that, the news media showed the police raiding a wedding in a church to arrest a suspect, and dragging him away from his weeping bride. The literature is also rife with incidents of this sort of atrocity, in spite of the fact that the Constitution of the United States designates places of worship as safe havens, inviolable from the forces of law, unless invited in, or to protect occupants from imminent danger.

Notwithstanding the Branch Dividian Compounds of the world, and maybe because of them, one learns the lesson of the resolve to protect one's religion and the lengths to which the disciples will go to protect God's temple. The Jews would never allow the aforementioned bombings of their holy places to go unpunished. Nor would they wait for the authorities to spend years investigating. They would take matters into their own hands.

The Moslems and other groups would retaliate without regard to being branded "terrorists" because they would consider it the ultimate sacrifice to die protecting the dwelling places of their faiths. African Americans must defend their churches and mosques with the same fervor as others do, and not allow these racist terrorists to prevail.

But the fervor to defend the church in the Black community should go even deeper. The church is the predominant and preeminent institution in this community. If the church is destroyed, then the community is destroyed. These arsonists know it.

Let's look at the role of the church in more detail. It has been the one institution that the chattel slave had been allowed to embrace, and every reasonable person knows why. The church was used, by the slave-master, to justify his inhumanity to people of color, and to promote his "white" God who (in His penultimate wisdom) ordained that they serve their master during the days of their lives. If he became a "good" slave, then he would be rewarded in heaven upon his death. *Of course the slave would end up in the black part of heaven*. The slave-master hired White preachers to spread this doctrine.

They later allowed some of the "good" slaves to learn the correct passages in the Bible and to teach their fellow slaves. Since slaves were barred from learning to read, under penalty of death, the Black preachers had no way of verifying the Bible's edict.

Fortunately, many of the slave preachers double-crossed the masters who had such "faith" in them. An example is Nat Turner, who used his freedom of movement as a preacher to plan a revolt to kill the masters and free many of the slaves from bondage. There are many other examples of slaves turning the tables and using the slave-masters' "design" to enhance the cause of manumission.

The antebellum black church-members learned to use codes to inform one another of the departure of the underground railroad passengers, to signal the "massa's" movement, to relieve the burdens of slavery by entertainment and relaxation, and to get and send messages to loved ones who had been "sold down the river." There are even churches where the slaves were taught to read, clandestinely.

With the end of slavery, the church became the center of social activities. It was the place where people gathered to share information concerning the plans the government had for the newly-freed persons, including programs designed to help them make the transition from slave to freed-man. The church socials allowed for recreation and as a meeting place for young and old people who wanted to acquaint or reacquaint themselves with one another. It provided a contact point for relatives who had been lost by the "institution" and had no other means of making contact. It provided the first schools to teach the heretofore illiterate chattels how to read and write, as well as organizing training venues to learn updated skills which could be used to eke out a "living". The church helped in organizing the voter education and became polling sites for the new voters as well as being information centers where these newly "elected officials" could meet with new constituents.

During the early post-bellum period when carpet-bagging and lynching were the ways of the South, the church again was the source of information and refuge. It provided the support and leadership in the African American community and it was a bulwark against the seemingly insurmountable oppression of the time.

The ministers were the preeminent community leaders, giving support, guidance and counsel to the masses.

As time progressed, the church became even more important in the life of the community. During the so-called civil rights era, it was the leadership of the church that sparked the flame of change. Although it was the action of Rosa Parks (when she refused to sit in the back of the bus) which lit the flame of change, it was the Southern Christian Leadership Conference that led the bandwagon, which others jumped on. It was a Southern Baptist minister, named Dr. Martin Luther King, Jr., who was drafted to launch the church's influence to a national and an international level in forging the change, which was to later come, in terms of what African Americans can do and where they can do it.

Although there were many other non-sectarian groups involved in the civil rights movement, none were anywhere as successful or influential as the religious groups.

It should be very clear that the use of "church" includes all the religious institutions to which Black Americans belong. Not to be forgotten is the fact that the Nation of Islam was very involved in the liberation struggle—on many fronts. Their premier spokesman, Malcolm X, might have been almost as important as Dr. King in "negotiating" change. It is believed that it was the specter of Malcolm X and his "by any means necessary" doctrine, which partially influenced the "powers that be" to acquiesce to Dr. King's demands. They did that, rather than face the "venom" of Malcolm X's followers and others, such as the Black Panther Party and the SNCC.

The church, then, was the rallying point for the civil rights movement and it was that institution which was mostly recognized by all as the axis of change, as well as the rock of stability, in the Black community. That is the reason why it is the institution now under physical attack by those who seek to stymie the progress of Africans on the continent and in the diaspora.

The enemies of liberation were very happy when, during the post-civil rights era, the church fell asleep. They were ecstatic when it fell into a coma and lost its vision and its leadership. They danced in the streets when the ministers became politicians and sold their souls to the highest bidders from the special interest groups.

The "leaders" were told they could reap for themselves, rather than be concerned about saving their flocks. So the masses fell into the precipice of despair, helplessness, hopelessness, drug abuse, sexual promiscuity, prostitution, and blindness.

So the church has changed, drastically, over the years. Or, maybe we should say that what we know about the church is drastically different from what we expect of it.

First of all, it abdicated its role as the moral leader of society. Leaders are morally bankrupt and, instead of leading their flocks to the path of righteousness, they rape and abuse young children and lead them down the path of damnation.

Witness the recent revelations of the Catholic Church's scandal, where hundreds of clerics have been accused, and many confessed to acts of abominations against children and against their "vows." Reflect on the scandals of the orphan British children sent to Australia in the 1940s who were made slaves and "holes" to the priests who were supposed to protect them. The scandals are too numerous to mention here but most of the information is available for public scrutiny.

While the Catholic church is the focus of current scrutiny, these same acts of depravity are occurring in most churches and denominations. This author has heard of many cases, including one where a Church of God minister was heard responding to a little boy's protest that what he was doing was wrong, by saying, "It's okay. I'm just giving you some fatherly affection." I have also had a minister who was accused of giving boys more than religious instructions.

In discussions with many people (including ministers of the gospel) about the apparent lack of moral suasion in the ministry, the most common response is that clerics are human, too. True! However, this author's belief is that those who present themselves as representatives of, and intercessors to God, should not, and must not, act as ordinary human beings. One would not expect a policeman or a judge to be a criminal (although many of them are), so one should not expect a minister to be a blatant sinner.

As mentioned earlier, the church has become a "cash-cow" for some of the new-fangled ministers. The ministers have become the conspicuous consumers of the late twentieth and early twenty-first centuries. Starting with the Rev. Ikes, their religion became the mighty dollar and how many they could accumulate. God became secondary and now there are ministers who boast about how many homes they have, how many cars, how expensive their suits, shoes and watches are, and what the name brands are. They take the rent money and the money their parishioners need to feed the children and, while they have much more than they can spend in a lifetime, the children of the church members are hungry and, sometimes, homeless. But the ministers admonish them to give more and have faith that the Lord will bless them even more.

The problem is that there are so many of them who are rotten to the core and who people believe in so fervently.

The people need to get involved in their churches, assess the roles of ministers and other religious leaders and where necessary, clean up the "house" by getting rid of those leaders who are acting in their own self-interest instead of the interest of the "flock."

They need to demand that their ministers have a "liberation" mentality and support those persons who are so bent.

The church needs to get involved in the community by "adopting" needy people and helping with their physical and spiritual well-being (without demanding "conversion" as a reward for those services). It needs to get involved in the community by sponsoring group homes for the aged, for children, for the homeless, and others in need of services. It should be a place of last refuge.

The church needs to continue its political activism, without having ministers become politicians. A true minister cannot be a true, successful, political representative of the people. The two professions are exclusive of one another if there is to be true success. The minister should be the spark in identifying and supporting a politician whom he/she truly believes will work in the interest of the community, and for no other reason, including that politician's support of that individual religious organization. The minister should be politically savvy and forward-looking.

The church should align itself with the educational institutions in a non-sectarian way. It should offer its teachers (including retirees) to help children who are struggling in school and should mobilize its members to mentor children and young adults in the ways of the world and teach them the secrets of success. There is an example of how the church can reach out. This is the "Manhood Program" (MAAFA) conducted by Rev. Johnny Ray Youngblood in East New York, in Brooklyn, New York.

There are many people in churches who have the wherewithal to reach out and adopt some of the many thousands of homeless and parent-less African children in America. Why is that not being done? We have abandoned our traditions of the extended family and now we are afraid of our children. We must have the nerve and the guts to reclaim them, as Jesus said "gather the little children...."

They are the most precious jewels and, if we are to save ourselves, we must save and preserve them.

Church members, led by ministers, must volunteer to help people in the community. A large percentage of active church members are retired persons. They need to volunteer maybe two to three hours a week to help anyone in need in the community. They can pass on their knowledge to other people, be it professional of otherwise. These people are, or have been, bankers, businesspersons, professional nurses, doctors, lawyers, builders, accountants, etc., and there are people in the community who need the types of training and/or advice which they can give but might not have the wherewithal to pay for the training or the information. Ministers need to pay attention and be the conduit to this kind of positive interaction.

There is much talk about "faith-based initiatives" which the governments, at all levels, seem to be funding these days. Although there seems to be a deliberate attempt by the progenitors of these programs to muddy the water with regard to the separation of church and state, some of these programs can be beneficial to the community and must be explored by these "liberation" ministers.

"Because the leaders have no vision, the people perish." A religious leader must be expected to have two types of vision. If a person is really "called to service" he/she should have the "vision from God." This vision includes divine guidance in terms of making the right religious decisions for the congregation. This vision entails an influence of the congregation to do good work for the upliftment of the moral and religious ethics of the community.

The other vision that a religious person should have is the vision to promote the physical welfare of the community. Hungry and deprived people in a community riddled with drugs and crime, are not good candidates for religion.

It is the role of the religious leader to influence the promotion of the social welfare of his/her congregation and community. This means that this leader should be involved in the schools, the policing, the politics, social service, and any other area that influences the congregants' lives.

In the years following the civil rights movement, there was a gap in the church and community, alike. The community had no leaders and the racists began a methodical effort to retrieve the "benefits" which they perceive to have been given to an inferior underclass which has no "rights" to them.

They began their assault on the "affirmative action" program that was designed to "level out the playing field" for so-called minorities. The Bakke case is one example. This man claimed that he encountered reverse discrimination because he was excluded from a college that admitted a black person who scored lower on the entrance exam than he, in order to fulfill a quota.

That may be the case, but what was being ignored is the fact that Blacks were, heretofore, not being let in because of who they were, notwithstanding how high they would have scored. Furthermore, Bakke's entry would not necessarily be guaranteed even if he was up against another White student, because test scores are not the only deciding factors in college admission, anyway.

They have also dismantled the laws governing set-aside programs in the many areas which would open the doors to African Americans, and allow some of the past exclusions to be addressed and future opportunities to be availed, either because the leaders have been bought, or they are asleep.

Fortunately, the time has arrived, once more, when the church is waking up. Some of the leadership is becoming aware of the tremendous downturn of the fortunes in the community and the need to stop the snowballing. These people have awakened from their deep slumber and, although they seem still in a daze, they have determined to do something about this dire situation.

Over years, many grass-root leaders, including Rev. Herbert Daughtry, Rev. Johnny Ray Youngblood, Rev. Dennis Dillon, and Rev. William Augustus Jones, among many others—in Brooklyn, New York and Father Lucas, the "rebel" Catholic priest have been crying in the wilderness, lamenting the church's abandonment of its responsibilities to the community. But it was Dr. Benjamin Chavis (later Benjamin Muhammad) who, while head of the NAACP, played the role which allowed for the summoning of over one million men to Washington, DC, by Minister Louis Farrakhan and has set the stage for the rejuvenation of the Church in the African American village.

And they burned the churches! What significance do these acts of desecration have? They are in direct reaction to the rejuvenated role of some of the churches in the African American community.

The arsonists, and others like them, are running scared. They have realized that many church leaders now understand that their constituents, as well as themselves, are losing ground, and so there is a call to arms to re-fight the battle for equality in the U.S.A., as well as world-wide. They figure that attacks on the holiest places in the community will demoralize the populace and sap the fighting spirit. These arsonists should be made to know that this will only redouble the effort to defend those places, and they should be made to pay, dearly.

The church continues to have an invaluable role to play in the African American community. It is the clergy that has the preparation and the moral suasion to guide the population towards the light of equality and success. It is in the church that one finds the wide variety of thought and ability that is necessary to come together to form the nucleus of the new freedom movement. It is the church that has the economic ability to change the lives of the common person, through its decisions on the banking institutions to use and the investments to make.

A good example has been set for the clergy by the Concerned Black Clergy group in Atlanta, Georgia, which, some years ago, decided to transfer millions of dollars in deposit from the traditional banks to a number of Black banks.

Let us consider the impact of that decision. The first benefit is that these banks are strengthened, thereby lessening the possibility of their "failures." This strengthening of these institutions is important because their success is critical in that it sets an example to the would-be entrepreneur that it can be done. The second benefit is that the funds are retained in these self-same community institutions, thereby keeping a larger portion of the financial resources in the community.

Benefit number three is that this money, which has been deposited in neighborhood institutions, now becomes available for loans to local businesses and individuals and will be a help in the revitalization of the area. More jobs can now be provided within that sector, not only through the banks' hiring of new personnel, but by the hiring of extra personnel by the borrowers, who will expand their investments and will need other goods and services.

This sort of resolve and sound financial thinking can be expanded to other religious institutions and organizations. For example, it is a disgrace that an organization like the National Baptist Convention, which is reputed to have over six million members, is financially impotent. Whether or not this figure is correct, imagine the tremendous clout that organization could exercise! If each member was asked to contribute one hundred dollars per year, specifically earmarked for the building or renovation of hotels in strategic cities, the organization's conventions (national and regional) could be held at these venues. An average contribution of two hundred dollars per year would have a multiplier effect, which would cause a geometric value additive.

Furthermore, other less financially sound organizations could utilize these places to have their meetings and could also be inspired to build their own. Tony Brown has suggested, on many occasions, the disgrace of these organizations spending billions of dollars every year renting space in European American hotels to have conventions when there is so much money available to have our own. He is right!

Adopt-a-Business

The church has, and can continue to, advance the economic standing of its congregation by doing some simple things to encourage the congregation to build the community from within. One simple act is to adopt-a-business in each of the general areas of need. That is, whatever one would ordinarily need to purchase, a committee might be appointed to identify a business that supplies that commodity or service. The following is the proposal for adopting a business:

"ADOPT A BUSINESS" PLAN

In light of the state of affairs with which people of African descent are faced, we must pull ourselves up by the proverbial "bootstraps." The only way to do that is to take advantage of our potential economic power by building and supporting our own community organizations, including businesses. To that end, a most appropriate means of community building will be the "adopt-a-business" concept. Adopting a business would mean supporting and promoting that business and helping to guarantee its success. Although conceptualized for adoption by a church, it is just as effective for use by any other organization or group of individuals.

The group and the businessperson should be both knowledgeable participants in the project. In the case of a church, a voucher can be issued to the church member who purchases goods from the business. A copy of this voucher should be retained by the business, with the second copy being issued to the purchaser, to be given to the church.

Every three months, or so, the business entity will add up the amount of the vouchers and issue a check to the church in the amount of about 5% of the amount of the sales. This money can then be used in the church, probably for the young people's endeavors or, if the businessperson supplies things that the church uses, then a combination of value and cash can be secured.

This can also be done in the case of sororities, fraternities, and other groups of individuals coming together for such a project. Support and promote also include individuals with contacts getting the information on the adopted business to other organizations, the media, and other individuals.

The businessperson also has responsibilities. First of all, he/she must know that a certain level of service and courtesy is demanded, as well as the reduction of prices when the level of growth has allowed for volume discount increases from suppliers. Furthermore, there should be the expectation that new staff should at least come partly from friends and relatives of the supporters, where feasible, and the business should otherwise become "a part of the community."

There is no reason that each group cannot adopt several businesses that supply different commodities. If enough of these adoptions take place, businesses in our community will become viable and we can build the community from within, without having to rely on what "other people" do for us.

Pay It Forward

The church is fertile ground for the concept of "Pay It Forward." Under this concept, the first person selects someone to help. It may be one or more persons. The idea is that the performer of the good deed does not require any compensation for that deed. Instead, the recipient is requested to pass on the good deed to others.

An example of the deed is that a person who is able, may pay for a youngster to attend college. The expectation is that once that youngster has completed his/her course of study and has secured a decent source of funds, then he/she must help a new person in like manner.

Maybe one person is unable to afford such a huge outlay, but is able to entice a group of friends and relatives to contribute. The same effect is garnered and the same expectation is had of the recipient.

Many churches have scholarship funds. Young people are afforded or helped to afford the privilege of going to college. They should be encouraged to give the same opportunity to another youngster when they have begun to earn. It is important that churches continue with that help, but that they also attach strings. The string to attach is the "Pay-it-Forward."

There is an infinitesimal number of good deeds which should be passed on from one to another and can be invaluable to the community through the pay-it-forward idea.

The above example is an expensive proposition, but the good deed may be as simple as helping someone to get a job, or providing help with one's rent, or helping someone pay funeral expenses.

Paying it forward creates a ripple effect that can have an unbelievably astounding positive effect on the community, which can sweep in even unknowing and unbelieving folks. That will help to recreate the family we once had as our support system and help to strengthen the foundation we need for rebuilding our past glory.

Promote Adoptions

Too many of our innocent children are stuck in drab, non-inspiring, dead-end group homes, or are homeless, helpless beings. This cannot be allowed to stand.

Too many mothers are left to care for little children because fathers have abandoned them or have been killed or are in prison, and they don't know what to do! These children need assistance. What is the Church going to do about them?

Churches need to set up adoption and welfare committees to identify children in need and match them with potential adoptive parents. In cases where a person may have the mind but not the means to adopt, others may have to "lend a hand" to make it happen. Of course, it is well known that the powers-that-be seem to prefer group homes to adoption, but the churches need to flex their muscles and insist that rules be changed, as necessary, to make sure that our children have loving, nurturing homes in which to live.

Some church members who want to have the children but cannot afford to adopt, should be assisted in becoming foster parents, with other parishioners being "aunts" and "uncles." If there is a commitment and a cooperation within the church and the community, most of our children can have "warm" and "comfortable" homes.

Mentoring

African Americans have adopted the misguided concept of the nuclear family, with tragic consequences. This has damaged the idea of the extended family, and the idea that it takes a whole village to raise a child. It's mostly because we have destroyed that value why we're floundering, so badly, in a sea of abyss, and don't know where we are going.

The Church needs to play the lead role in acting as a guiding light for our youth (within and outside of the Church) by organizing mentoring programs for our youth, especially the boys. They are at high risk of extinction.

Mentoring takes many different forms and almost everyone in a church can be a mentor. For example, a child may just need help with homework. There's a mentor for that! He/she may have problems at home or at school. There's a mentor for that! Children may need a big brother or a big sister to help guide them along the path of life. They may be involved with sports or the arts, and need a mentor. They may be attending, or planning to attend college, or taking a job, and they need a mentor for that. They may have lost their parents and need a mentor; or become hooked on drugs, and need some help and guidance out of the belly of darkness, and need a mentor for that!

And it is not just children who need mentors. Many adults need them, too, including alcoholics and other drug abusers, injured veterans, and many others.

Mentoring can also be rewarding for the mentor, the least being the satisfaction one obtains in helping others. There is even the belief that those who help others live a longer, happier life. But the mentor helps him/herself in many other ways. He or she may have to do "research" in order to assist the mentee, and may find that experience to be educational. They may have to travel to new places and see new things. The mentee may be given grants or other funds, or meet "important" people, from which the mentor garners benefits.

There is an old adage, which says that when one gives freely one receives value ten-fold. Mentoring is a case that gives truth to that adage and church folk must get involved in it, vigorously. Besides, by mentoring, the church is strengthening its members and, therefore, itself.

There are many things that the church can do, and the number is only limited by the imagination of the leaders and the congregations. The only thing that this author will insist on, is that the leaders of the church realize that the strength of the church rests on their shoulders, and that strength determines what it can do for its community. What the church does for the community will determine how strong the community is, and whether it survives, because most people recognize the church as the "rock" of any community.

Section IV

Political Impact

Above all the impotencies that the African American community suffers, perhaps none is more devastating than the political lynching of the race.

And let us understand what I mean by lynching. There are many misused words in the English vocabulary, but this one describes the effect of the doctrine of a certain man named Willie Lynch (see *Introduction*).

Mr. Lynch was, allegedly, a consultant to white southern slave-masters. He admonished against physical injury to their expensive "property", and suggested a means of indoctrination that led to the Josh-Sambo syndrome. The method used was to get Josh by himself, tell him he was a good man, and apologize for being forced to enslave him. The promise was made to treat him as well as possible in recognizing his human-ness. Josh was told that part of his problem was no-good slaves like Sambo, the scum of the earth, who were always ostracizing good people like Josh and telling lies on them. He was, finally, asked to help keep Sambo in check by reporting his activities so that less retribution would be heaped upon him and his other fellows-in-bondage.

Sambo was similarly summoned at some other time, admonished and encouraged to spy on Josh.

Over a hundred-and-fifty years after the end of "slavery", and at a point where we should have learned that our only hope for survival and progress is in cooperation, we seem to be doing everything in our power to perpetuate the Josh-Sambo syndrome.

You may ask how that is relevant to our political plight? Just read on, and you will see. At a time when we are strong in numbers, and particularly potentially powerful in some quarters, we do not have enough faith in one another (or maybe we are not astute enough) to cooperate politically. If we need to know how we should "work it" we should take a page from the book of the Jews. The fact is less than two million Jews control New York City and less than five million American Jews practically control the United States. How do they do it? They learn how the system works and then they vote in blocks.

The Jewish "community" has taught us (if we wish to learn) that a small group can control what the larger group does, if it is politically astute. Let's see what they do!

They first vote for their own. When one is running against a Gentile, that one gets the vote, regardless of the level of qualification of the different candidates. The edict, "above all, to thine own self be true" is activated. The now elected official fights for and furthers the agenda of the group in every possible way. S/he keeps the community informed at all times and seeks feedback as to the best course of action when conflicts arise. S/he seeks and finds jobs within the governmental structure at all levels for the constituents and is willing to cry anti-Semitism if someone dares to disagree, or to criticize the course of action.

This representative is willing and able to stand on the picket line alongside the represented constituents, for whatever reason a picket line is set up, and though I know that they sometimes disagree with actions and/or methodology, they almost never publicly criticize one another.

They are not afraid to take their colleagues to task on matters of importance to their constituency because, to them, that constituency is predominant. They are also willing to make alliances when it is in their best interests to do so.

Although the Jews are the most pronounced in their racial (religious?) togetherness, most other groups also solidify to promote their self-interest. It seems that all groups do that, except for the African, at home or in the diaspora.

If we are to make progress, the first thing we must do is "learn" the political system. It is many-tiered, with each level of government being responsible for different needs of the individual American.

The Federal government is responsible for some services, the state for some others, and the local government for the rest of the services. It is the local government that has the most impact on the day-to-day life of the individual, although most people believe that it is the Federal government. So they hold their Congressman responsible for all the ills which they suffer. Come on folks. Get with it!

This is not intended to be a civics lesson so I encourage readers to do more research in that area. However, I will now give you a brief outline of the realities of the American government.

Federal Government

The Federal government is made up of the Presidency, a Bicameral Legislature, and the Supreme Court. The President is elected every four years and is very important in the scheme of things. He is the chief enforcer of the laws. We will deal with that matter later. The Supreme Court interprets the law, and is sometimes known to "make" laws by its interpretation. The Legislature is made up of the two Houses of Congress—the Senate and the House of Representatives. The members of the House are commonly called Congressmen, and are usually the people blamed for all the ills of the country.

Aside from making laws, the Congress is responsible for overseeing the collection and disbursement of Federal taxes. This disbursement is done in the form of entitlements to individuals, as well as Block Grants and Revenue Sharing with the States.

The Federal government has policing duties, both at home and at its borders. Very important, in the scheme of things, is the drug policies, especially with regard to guarding its borders and punishing drug dealers at all levels.

Immigration policies have come into question, of late, especially the so-called Southern Hemisphere Restrictions. Under this policy, peoples of the Southern Hemisphere of the world, who are mostly people of color, are being restricted from migrating to the United States, while those from the Northern Hemisphere (mostly white) are being encouraged to come here.

The Federal courts play a major role in the life of the people of the United States. It is the arbitrator of last resort, when the local and state courts have failed to dispense "justice". However, the ability of the Republican presidents—over an eighteen-year period—to stack the courts with conservative, "right-wing" radicals, there is now a lack of protection in the Federal courts for people of color, in particular, and poor people, in general.

At the Supreme Court level, we have seen Affirmative Action shot down on many fronts, and left smoldering in the dust. We have seen police at all levels given the green light to violate all the rights heretofore guaranteed by the Bill of Rights of the Constitution. All citizens stand to lose from the ebbing of these protections, but people of color are the most vulnerable. Add the new "homeland security" hubbub to the mix, and we become more solidly entrenched "behind the eight ball."

State Government

The State government is made up of a Governor, a Bicameral Legislature (Senate and Assembly), and the Court system. The duties of these three entities are somewhat similar to those at the Federal level, except that the State should not engage in foreign policy. Nor is the State responsible for interstate commerce.

The State is responsible for regulating things such as marriage, automobile registration, and the like, in addition to having some of the responsibilities for collecting and disbursing state (and, sometimes local) taxes. The State operates certain agencies which have direct benefits to the local communities, but most of its contributions are done through revenue-sharing, whereby it gives back some of the taxes it collects, to the local governments.

This is not always done in an equitable manner. For example, whereas New York City contributes significantly more than half of New

York State's revenue, it gets back significantly less than half of the revenue shared. This is partly because many New York City representatives in State government vote along with their upstate cronies to "do-in" the city. It is also partly because the census figures under-represents the New York City population (the "hidden" hundreds of thousands are not counted), thus allowing the city fewer representatives than it is entitled.

Reason three for this discrepancy is that the up-staters do not like the New York City dwellers, partly because they are mostly so-called minorities, and they feel that they can do whatever they wish because those residents won't fight back.

An example of this (which was mentioned previously) is the fact that they pass laws which calls for certain restrictions on the rights of cities with "over one million population." New York City is the only one in New York with more than one million population, so that it is enjoined from requiring residency for its uniformed employees, whereas every other county or city in the state can require residency. That is unconstitutional, because all the residents of a state must be treated equally, and if one is allowed, all should be allowed. Similarly, if one is enjoined, all should be enjoined.

The State is also responsible for its law enforcement. Therefore, there is the State Police, as well as State Courts, which are used in this vein.

Local Government

Local government structures vary, depending on where one resides. In most places, there is a county government that supersedes a city government or a town council. In New York City, however, there are five counties that are subordinate to the City government. The local government is the entity responsible for one's everyday quality of life issues. It is responsible for the infrastructure (roads, sanitation facilities, social welfare, schools, police and fire services, etc.). The mayors or county leaders have significant influence on which citizens obtain the services for which they pay taxes. It is at this level that the majority of the abuses, which are heaped on citizens, occur.

The Electoral Process

One has only to watch comedian Jay Leno's "Jaywalking" on the "Tonight Show" to realize the naïveté of the average American with regard to things, in general, but politics, in particular. Very few have the faintest clue about how the political process works, who their representatives are, or what is represented. Those who go to the polling sites cast their votes based on who they like, who the media says is leading in the polls, or who they dislike based on whether they had sex or not, or if they believe the person wants the appearance of "equality" for all Americans.

While it is true that Leno is a comedian, the facts cannot be denied that a great number of people seem to be ignorant of what's happening in the world. This was very evident in the presidential elections of the year 2000, where the well-connected George W. Bush, son of the well-connected former president, was "appointed" president of the United States.

The Constitution of the United States demarcates certain rules for electing persons to office in the various positions. The different states have enacted legislation for electing candidates based on the federal model, which should not be in violation of those federal election laws.

The rules call for primary elections to be held to select candidates for each "party" position that is opposed, and then a general election to determine the winner of the opposing party candidates. This is consistent, regardless of the level of the office that is sought.

As intimated, states have some leeway in terms of deciding the electoral process. Although there may be benefits to this (this author cannot find them), there are tremendous drawbacks. This discrepancy was blatant in the year 2000 presidential election where the Florida ballots were "gerrymandered" in order to help appoint GW to the presidency. This was done in spite of the fact that Al Gore got the majority vote and would have won Florida by a landslide if so many people of color were not disenfranchised by their vote being discounted based what was, undoubtedly, fraud.

The Florida fiasco has highlighted the fact that the electoral process has to be federalized and made consistent from state to state. All votes should be counted in every election because that is what every citizen should expect and demand.

There are other states, such as Georgia, which are in violation of the one-man-one-vote rule. For example, people are registered as Democrats or Republicans, with the understanding that they hold specific ideas and party affiliations.

It is an injustice to a voter from either party (or a third party) to have someone influence the selection of the representative from your party to compete with their party candidate in a general election. Intelligence dictates that they will help to select the person whom their party is expected to beat in a general election, or the one who most closely represents their own ideology, rather than the ideology of the party "faithfuls". This does not allow the party faithfuls to truly select the representatives of their choice, and their agenda is threatened or eliminated by this miscarriage of justice.

The above-mentioned, unconstitutional, act of allowing non-party voters to vote in a party's primary, has been shown to have negative effects for the party candidate, as personified by the removal from office of Representative McKinney of Georgia, because the "good ole boys" had been unhappy with her speeches and activity.

The Presidency

The President is head of the Executive Branch of the government of the United States. Whereas the Congress passes the laws and the Courts interpret them, it is he who is the enforcement officer of the country. The three branches of the government are to each provide a check and balance to others, but the other branches have allowed the president to run rough-shod over them, especially in the past few years. The president is also the representative of the country to the world and recommends foreign policy, as well as domestic policy actions to the Congress which, in turn, acts on legislation.

Political Activism

Many of us call ourselves political activists. Some of us know what it means, and are even committed to the cause, notwithstanding the ramifications of our actions. Others do not understand the concept, so they are "activists" when it suits their purpose or they are part-time activists. True political activism means that one has to study politics and be committed to working through—or changing—the system in order to cause it to benefit the constituency for which one is "working."

As aforementioned, in order to benefit from a system—the first thing one has to do is to learn about the system. People often blame the President or their Congresspersons for problems that are to be solved locally. They also blame local politicians for problems that need national solutions.

So, now that you have a better understanding of how the government works, let us pursue some of the everyday activities and shortcomings of both the politicians and ourselves.

I have spoken with friends who lambaste former President Bill Clinton for not doing more for Black folks. After all, they reason, he could not have become president had it not been for the support, and vote, of African Americans. The question to be answered here is whether or not Bill Clinton is a friend of the people in our community.

I will start by saying that I was very angry when, prior to his election, he had the audacity to chide the NAACP (while speaking as a guest at their conference) about whom they should coddle, and for having Sister Souljah as their guest. That is comparable to a dinner guest telling the host that another dinner guest should be sent home without supper. That was an insult to the organization, in particular, and Black folks, in general. No one should be allowed to tell us who our friends should be, especially someone from outside, telling us to reject one of our own. While we may not agree with everything our own says and does, we have to agree to disagree and to lend advice and support to our brothers and sisters.

That having been said, we need to look at what he had done in terms of inclusion of African Americans, as well as other ethnic groups, in positions of authority within his government. What other president had African Americans as Secretaries of Departments. Others may have had one or two Assistant Secretaries, but Assistant Secretaries are like Vice Presidents—they carry out orders. He put his money where his mouth was. The naysayers who were opposed to him and say that he had not done enough should start looking at the opposition that he, and other leaders of goodwill, had constantly faced when people of color have been elevated. Does anyone have the illusion that some of the opposition he faced was not the result of his being seen as a "nigger-lover?"

I cannot get into the head of President Clinton in order to learn whether what he had tried to do in terms of inclusion of the many ethnic groups into government was based on altruism or common-sense. Some of us know that Abraham Lincoln has been celebrated as the Great Emancipator, but that he "freed" the Southern slaves as a means both to demoralize the South and to give the slaves a reason to ally themselves with the North and become "soldiers" for the Northern army. He, himself, is reputed to have uttered that if he could rejoin the union without freeing a single slave, he would have, but that was not possible. He also, supposedly, said that he would not sit at a table and break bread with a negro. The point is that we cannot correctly perceive the motive for anyone's actions. We must judge only the results.

The Bush regime since then jumped on his bandwagon in an effort to woo Black voters. This adds to the importance of what President Clinton has done.

The highlights of the presidency of Lyndon B. Johnson is the 1964 Civil Rights Act, as well as many other pieces of legislation which allowed people of color to be able to go to the bathroom, or restaurant, etc., in public places, without having to use the back door. While it is true that most of the benefits of those pieces of legislation accrued to women, homosexuals, and other diverse groups, the result is that certain burdens of Jim Crow laws were eased from our shoulders. *Our problem with respect to these gains is that we sought integration instead of equality, and we are no better off, especially financially.*

Should we continue to lambaste people such as President Clinton for how little they are doing for us, or should we use the limited opportunities such people present, in order to push the door wide open to opportunities? I say that we should jam a door-stop under those doors and let the multitude through. Only we can make it happen!

Most of us had followed the Lewinsky story and the December, 1998, impeachment charges against President Clinton. We heard the hullabaloo about his use of his power and influence over this innocent girl to make her do things to him which were improper. If we take proper stock of the situation, however, we must conclude that she *and* Linda Tripp were both culpable in this situation. So what outcome should that culpability have brought?

First of all, when he was asked whether or not he had been sexually involved with the young lady, he should have replied that he was answerable only to his wife. It is no one else's business. The Tripp woman should be the one to be prosecuted because she is the only one who broke the law. Clinton has a right to "protect" his family, by lying to everyone else, if necessary.

But all of these charges and countercharges have nothing to do with his tryst with Lewinsky. There was a faction that did not want to see him as president. As a commentator stated, with the Republican control of the White House for twenty of the previous twenty-four years, many people were put into places of influence, and they did not want to see the apple-cart overturned by the takeover by the Democratic party. They had been willing to do anything that it took to see that that didn't happen.

They tried "Filegate" and "Travelgate" and "White-water" and many other ruses to unseat that president. They tried indicting his Secretaries and, it is speculated, killed his Secretary of Commerce, and friend, Ron Brown. When all of these other attempts failed, they tried to bring him down using his "weakness" for women. They pursued him, in spite of the fact that they had their own weaknesses for women (and men), which were subsequently exposed.

Added to their resolve to remove President Clinton from office, was the fact that he started the "debate on racism." He went too far! He apologized for slavery and admonished Americans that all Americans should be treated with respect and *as* Americans, regardless of color or creed. How dare he!! He had to go! So the sinners cast their stones, notwithstanding the ricochets, and they apologized for their own sins and begged forgiveness, while condemning the president for his sins and saying that he was not penitent enough. And as they "bit the dust" they entreated him to fall with them;

their sacrifice was worth the price for preserving the white supremacy and the exclusion of others.

These same jackals who were stalking the president had nothing to say about President Reagan and his Vice President who ran drugs to get the money to buy arms to continue a war for which the Congress had cut off funding. Those actions were the "high crimes and misdemeanors" of which the Constitution spoke in consideration of removing a president from office. Not the lying about whether one had sexual relations with "that woman!"

As a matter of fact, when President Reagan died, all the accolades tempted one to join with the right-wingers, in declaring him a saint.

In 1994, the people of New York decided that Governor Mario Cuomo had outlived his usefulness. This charge was supported by people of color, either by their votes against him, or their failure to go to the polls. Was that decision good for New York? Was it good for people of color, especially people of African descent? The answer is a resounding no. True, Mario Cuomo did not show the appreciation he should for the support that Black voters had given him. True that he should have done more. True that he was short-sighted and, maybe, had bad advisors who underestimated the power of the Black vote. But who lost in the end?

Black voters had some access to Governor Cuomo through their representatives. This was not the case with his successor, George Pataki. Cuomo would listen to arguments concerning budget considerations that impacted the Black community. This was not the case with his successor. It was he who (at the urging of "minority" legislators) instituted the Curriculum of Inclusion in the State of New York. It was he who orchestrated and built a high-tech research institution in the state capital, over which his successor gloried.

True, he supervised the largest increase in prison space of any governor, and true, "minorities" are the largest inhabitants, but we live in a time when more crime is being committed and more people deserve to be incarcerated. (The down side is that a lot of innocent people are also caught up in the net.) What we need to do is to judge whether the pluses outweigh the minuses, and keep the person with more pluses than minuses. It was his successor, along with that stupid mayor of New York City, who asked Washington to decrease the amount of revenue sharing to the city and state, because they did not want to help the needy of the city—White or Black.

In 1993 the voters of New York City decided to support a racist and elect him as mayor. The hordes of African Americans sat on their fat asses at home and did not vote because they did not believe that Mayor Dinkins had done anything for them. They could not see what he had done for them, personally, so they decided that it didn't matter who was mayor, because "none of them does anything for me" anyway. It is that kind of thinking which now makes Black folks fear for our children and for ourselves on the street.

Four days after the election of this dictator, a group of police told Black people on Fulton Street, in Brooklyn—while beating a street vendor and covering their badges—"That boy, Dinkins, is gone. The street belongs to us, again." And did they ever mean it! People of color are literally under siege. I feel safer around criminals than around the police. One can fight back, or run from the criminal!

In July, 1998, I had a curious interaction with two police officers in New York City. I had failed to notice a sign which said "No left turn between....", and had made the turn only to be stopped by a White police officer. After presenting my driver's license, registration certificate and insurance card to him I explained that I had been vigilant but had not seen the sign. The fact is that I thought it curious that no other vehicles were turning so I looked at the many different signs in sight but had not spotted that one, so I thought it okay to turn since I had done so many times in the past.

I followed the policeman's instructions to pull over into a taxi stand where I was now delaying the flow of traffic while he went over to consult his partner. Being suspicious, as I am of all police officers, I asked my son to take over the wheel and I went to where they were having their discussion. I was surprised when the officer handed me my paperwork with the explanation that they believed that I had told the truth that I did not see the sign and then remarked that they were two of the good New York City policemen. It is only fair to add that my vehicle had Georgia tags because I commuted to and from that state, so they might have felt that they were "impressing" an out-of-towner. The point is that these policemen were acknowledging, even if unwittingly, the many negative actions of their colleagues.

The police have become more trigger-happy and more and more innocent people are being shot in the back. What's more, the judges are in cahoots with them. If they are indicted, all they do is request a trial by a judge who, invariably, set them free. The evil mayor—in all his splendor and intelligence—has said that everyone knows that he gave the police the benefit of the doubt in all cases. This should not be surprising because, as candidate for mayor, he incited a police riot at City Hall. The man is a criminal who belongs behind bars.

So what did Mayor Dinkins do for Black people? Let's look at his tenure. His election to the office heralded in a period of high hope for the community that, at long last, they would have access to, and be able to participate in, the governance of the City of New York. Mr. Dinkins, however, made many mistakes. He began by playing politics and keeping former Mayor Edward Koch's appointees in positions, probably because he knew them and thought that their experience would bode well for his administration. The problem with that thinking is that these people were Edward Koch's friends, not David Dinkins'.

The second mistake is that he tried too hard to please the press. The press was trying—and in many instances succeeded—in setting policy. They bullied him and pointed out every teeny "mistake" that he made, and when he didn't make any, they criticized his love of tennis, his immaculate way of dressing, or the bed he slept in.

The third thing he did wrong was that he tried to cater to a constituency that despised him, while outwardly ignoring the people who had got him elected. The Brooklyn people who had worked hard for him were ignored in his tour of the boroughs, while the good racists of Queens and Staten Island were wooed. He could not win those people's hearts, anyway, even if he gave them a million dollars each. In all fairness to him, there was a shooting in a Brooklyn high school on the day he should have toured a couple of the Brooklyn community board areas, but he did not reschedule.

The Crown Heights "riot" was his biggest blunder, however. Instead of being mayoral, making the proper decisions, and letting the chips fall where they may, he seemed to have sided with the Jewish community, although a speeding, drunken Jew had run over a small Black child, and fled the scene of the accident. The child died and the culprit is safely hidden away in Israel, someplace.

Having pointed out Mr. Dinkins' shortcomings, let me hasten to add that his election was the best thing that ever happened to New York City. The city, in general, and people of color, in particular, accrued great rewards.

Under his leadership, the Department of Business Services launched a campaign to include "minorities" in the city's contract process. Whereas Edward Koch was pressured to set aside 10% of the contracts for Minority and Women, David Dinkins set aside 14% for "minorities" and 9% for women. He also had the city guarantee bonding for those "minority" contractors who won bids. What is the importance of this?

Although there had been a 10% set-aside for "minority" and women under the previous administration, the White males would set their women up in business, and so the set-aside did not filter down to people of color. Furthermore, since most city contractors need to be bonded, and the bonding companies are almost all White-run, "minority" groups lost contracts because they could not obtain the crucial bonding. Under the Dinkins formula, all "minorities" could access the 14% and all women could access the 9% and, with the city's guarantee of bonding, one could not lose the contract because of failure to obtain the proper coverage.

The other crucial issue was the one dealing with a larger contractor's agreement to "cover" a small contractor and share in the profit. Under the old practice, the large contractor sometimes failed to do anything at all, but would sometimes get more than fifty percent of the profit. They would sometimes even get a qualified person to front for them and pay a percentage to that person. The bid, then, would be fraudulently misdirected.

Under the Dinkins plan, the major contractor would have to show that it rendered measurable assistance to the "minority" contractor and could not demand more than thirty-five percent of the profit. Bloomberg has eliminated it all.

With respect to the safety about which the Giuliani administration boasted, the praise should have gone to the past mayor. It was he who hired more police, orchestrated the "safe streets, safe cities" plan while the succeeding occupant of city hall was orchestrating a police riot in the city. He touted the value of the great mosaic that is New York City, while dispelling the myth of the melting pot. Part of the crime reduction effort also entailed entreating businesses to give youngsters summer jobs to get them off the street, as well as providing other avenues for recreation and creativity. This included refurbishing parks and playgrounds and building youth centers. The succeeding New York City mayor reversed all the gains.

In order to be proper activists we need to be able to analyze situations like the foregoing and to decide what benefits can accrue from our involvement in the political arena.

Since the so-called Civil Rights Era, hundreds of African Americans have been elected to office at the different levels of government. What benefits have accrued to the Black community as a result of this seeming increase in representation? What opportunities have we seized? What acts have we committed which have put us a step forward?

There is a group to which I belonged that was potentially very strong, indeed. In fact, its strength had been shown in a number of different ways.

The group was made up of Black elected Brooklyn officials—federal, state, and local—with each official appointing a number of supporters from each of their electoral districts. These persons served as advisors to all the elected representatives and brought many and varied perspectives to the group.

Throughout it's many years of existence, it managed to spearhead the election of many African Americans and Caribbean Americans to offices previously held by other groups, notwithstanding our majority numbers in these communities.

The organization had many years of struggle, and was under siege because it threatened the *status quo*. Even though the powers that be were unhappy with it, many White politicians had come before us each election season to seek our support of their candidacies. These vote seekers included statewide, citywide, and community based candidates for political offices and judgeships.

One would believe that an organization such as this would have the support of the Black community, in general, and Black politicians, in particular, but this was not always the case. Typically the Black politicians who sought our support wanted unconditional alliance and allegiance, but that couldn't be given. We didn't support and promote people solely because they were Black. They were interviewed concerning their motives for seeking office, their goals and their dreams for the community. Because every Black candidate who won an election in our Borough was a potential member of the organization, it was very important that the selected supportee be of good character and "conscience", with the same goals as the group.

Unfortunately, as Black folks are wont to do, some "rejected" candidates took it personally and declared war on us. But it was almost never personal with some of us. For example, there are many instances where there were warm feelings for the candidate, but the belief that the person could not win and, thereby, would allow for the victory of a person who was an "enemy" of the community precluded our support for that candidacy. There were a few instances when more than one member of the group sought to run for the same office. Whom does one support? Once again, the decision could not be based solely on personality. Of course, someone always ended up being sore at the group when such a difficult choice was made.

Every group is subject to the adverse effects of "group dynamics." Especially since this was a political organization, folks got ornery when one exerted "independence." There was the problem of the double-edged sword. Appointees were, to be sure, expected to vote "with" their sponsors, for the most part. But what about their consciences, or their own constituents? I believe, though, that notwithstanding these perceived pressures, most people voted the interest of their community.

The elected officials faced a different dilemma. There were a few who were interested only in promoting their own self-interests, so it didn't matter to them how the group voted on the various issues. They did their own thing. Most, though, were very hard-working, community-minded individuals. But how did they handle themselves when the group voted one way but they still needed to negotiate with their colleagues in order to get the service or restriction for their constituents?

Like any other organization, this one had functional problems. Decision-making by committee has never been the most efficient means of settling disputes or forming policy, but it is the way of a democratic society. Therefore, this organization, like others, had to come to grips with this reality.

Each member became involved because he or she believed that his or her opinion was important, and counted. It became very hard to subordinate one's opinions to others', which at times seems inferior (or at least less effective). The other problem with this form of decision-making process is that there are too many voices to be heard and too little time for each participant to detail an opinion or plan. Most committee persons, thus, end up frustrated by the outcome of most discussions.

Another problem is the fact that our recommendations were not binding, not even on our members-at-large. So people spent many hours debating and pondering, and "motivating" and voting and, in the end, it is mostly meaningless but for the exercise in rules of order—or disorder—as the case may be.

Regardless of what may be considered to be its shortcomings, organizations such as this one provides the building block for community development, for many reasons:

1. It was an organization that had crossed the boundary from talk to action and was *doing* something.

2. It acted as a role model for other organizations to pattern, both in terms of its failures and successes.

3. It had been able to bring together divergent thought processes and personality characteristics that seek to attain one goal, even if the means are sometimes contrary.

4. Its very existence acted as a catalyst to engender a higher level of respect for the community.

5. The anticipation of positive outcomes from interaction with such a group sometimes inspires politicians and other individuals and groups to act in a manner beneficial to the community.

6. The possible negative outcome of not cooperating with (or antagonizing) this type of group may cause some decision-makers to modify their actions.

7. The individual members benefit from the interaction with the group both for their own enlightenment and reinforcement and for the benefit of the other organizations to which they belong.

8. The hard work of the group—with the combined efforts of individual members providing the synergy—does pay dividends in geometric proportions.

It is from such an organization that the "grassroots" develops, strengthens, and makes changes to a community, empowering the people and shattering the *status quo*.

The importance of a group such as this became all the more clear after the September 9, 1997, primary elections in New York City when a group of negro "Republicrats" endorsed then incumbent mayor for re-election. It was not unexpected to see White so-called Democrats support the White racist mayor because they are the same people who worked undercover to defeat the Black Mayor Dinkins. But it is treason for these Black politicians to work against the interest of the community and the penalty for treason during war is death. Now, before the scavengers try to pick my bones for suggesting physical assassination, let me make myself clear. True, they deserve death, but that is not an option. The next best thing, therefore, is to declare them dead to the community and to destroy their careers, because they are more dangerous to us than the enemy without.

We cannot, however, be shocked at the treacherous acts of these mongrels! I'm reminded of a racist school superintendent with whom we had to deal when I was a member of the PTA executive board at my children's elementary school. He would publicly belittle Black parents in order to deflect attention from the fact that he catered only to the caucasian "side" of the district. However, whenever he became aware of parents who would not be bullied, he would either offer them a menial job with the district or agree to a few of their demands. The condition, however, was that they would be quiet and not let their colleagues at the other schools know what they were getting. He added that the recipients had earned these benefits and that there was not enough to give to all the schools. One may probably be surprised at how many PTA presidents "sold out" for these little crumbs.

In an effort to neutralize the only Black school board member, this superintendent made sure to "serve" him dinner at a school board retreat. The result was that the member later exclaimed "he is a very nice man, once you get to know him." The devil was also nice to Jesus when he tried to tempt him.

This same superintendent was reputed to tape the conversations which he had with people in his office and would steer the conversation in order to record his guests saying whatever he wanted them to "say." It became a rule of thumb for those of us who were so notified, not to meet alone with him.

I told this story in order to point out the fact that the house negroes have been co-opted either by threats, greed, or blindness. Whatever the cause, they have been lost to us and we must excise them. They are a cancer that must be eliminated before it kills the group.

Notwithstanding the foregoing conclusions about the need to eliminate certain people from our midst, it is only fair to say that not all of them are bad people. Some of them truly believe that they are doing the right thing, but they are either stupid or mis-educated. Some of the people who supported the New York City mayor in the 1997 election did so to protect their "programs" which they knew he would destroy if he was re-elected and they did not vote for him. And they were right! He and his cronies dismantled community-based organizations through strong-armed tactics and fear. (This matter is further discussed elsewhere.) Unfortunately, the vast majority of these otherwise good people cannot, and will not change, so we cannot be influenced by their good intentions if they are a danger to the race.

The foregoing are people who will argue that "law and order" praise is essential in the Black community, so it's okay for the police to harass, brutalize, and kill innocent men, women, and children because the police will be feared, and that will reduce crime. But what about respect for the police? Will that not reduce crime more effectively? They praised a mayor who put back $50 million into the Board of Education budget—in an election year—to "buy well-needed textbooks" as pro-education and sensitive to the needs of public school children. The problem is that he is the one who caused the crisis, in the first place, by taking more than $1 billion from the same school budget.

Unfortunately, many of the people whom the group helped to get elected, succumbed to the human frailties of greed, stubbornness and stupidity. At the last meeting which I attended, there was a discussion that, since one of our members had become county leader, we no longer should "agitate" for our rights because it would make him look bad and even weaken his position. They could not reason that the group was the important entity, not the individual and, in fact, our agitation could have strengthened his hand. (The irony is that the powers that be accused the Black county leader of wrongdoing, indicted him and sent him to prison.)

Some elected members were not happy that their actions were subject to scrutiny. They were more often absent from meetings. They did not always follow recommendations of the group, either.

There were some other elected officials who did not want the organization to continue, because they wanted to crown their offspring as their successors, and so they weakened the organization.

The result is that it died! And with it the hard work and aspirations of many community leaders who had put in thousands of hours of valuable time and effort to build, and leave, a political legacy for the generations. The wheel must, once again, be reinvented! African Americans must, once again, go to the powers that be to beg on our knees, instead of having them come to us, with hats in hands and promises galore. There were some good, visionary, politicians, who started the organization under discussion, and they will continue to do good work, but others should be chastised.

The 1997 Democratic Primary election in New York City was a revealing one, not so much for what happened during the election, but what happened afterwards.

As usual, there had been cries of irregularities, and this is par for the course in that city where election corruption is the order of the day.

The news, however, centered around the "colored" Republicrats who had deserted the Democratic Party and the African American community. So what was the story behind these rats deserting what they construed as a sinking ship which they helped to sink? This author can only speculate, based on the facts that presented themselves.

The surveys and polls presented in the media told the story of the re-election of Herr Giuiliani as mayor of the city. This mayor had been well-known for his bully tactics and for severely punishing his "enemies." His enemies included not only those who opposed him, but those who disagreed with anything he did or said. Furthermore, his wrath extended to his own people who dared to overshadow him and he was not afraid to break the law in order to mete out punishment. Then when he was brought to task for breaking the law, he said, "There are so many obscure laws that one cannot be expected to know and obey all of them." Yet he wanted to punish citizens for not obeying even things which are not the law but what he thought should be. An example of his disregard for the law was his withholding of funds from a couple of City Council persons who opposed him, even though he had no legal authority to do so. However, the message was received and City Councilpersons, as well as others, began to acquiesce to his wishes in order not to be punished.

So here was the scenario: The people who foretold the re-election of the tyrant mayor hedged their bets, figuring that if they supported him he would be nice to them in the next term.

While in a bank one day, I actually heard one Black fool verbalize this ridiculous sentiment to his friend, "the reason he was against us in the first term was because we did not vote for him." He added that if we didn't vote for him we couldn't expect him to do anything for us. So he was making sure to go and cast his vote for the incumbent mayor.

The support for this man from the then City Councilperson from Central Brooklyn was no surprise to anyone. She had no allegiance to anyone except herself and she would sell her soul to the devil if she thought that she could get some publicity or a job for a family member. The surprising thing was that the labor union representatives supported a man who has consistently displayed anti-union sentiments throughout his career—except for the police who he used to carry out his evil deeds. In fact, there was lot of grumbling within DC 37 union and elsewhere, over the endorsements.

Endorsements by two African American Congressmen were, by far, the most shocking insults to the community.

On two occasions, the residents of New York City voted for their representatives to be elected to the respective offices for no more than two four-year terms. After the 9/11 attack Guiliani attempted to overturn that limit by arguing that he was the best person to continue leading the city after the catastrophe. His arguments were rejected.

Eight years later, "Napoleon" Bloomberg hijacked democracy in NYC by bribing and cajoling his fellow lame-duck elected officials in the City Council to overturn term limits. The decision was supported by state officials. Where was the Governor? That act set a terrible precedence in this country and should not be allowed to stand. Power corrupts and absolute power, which people like him seek, corrupts absolutely.

We are duty bound, to ourselves, to our family, and to our community, to look at the political decisions we make and the people we support for office. We must realize that we put people there (if we vote) and, therefore, they work for us. We should fire them if they don't act in our interest.

The Police

The police, as aforementioned, take their cue from their leader and act as they interpret his edict on law enforcement. A classic example of this is the case of a White police commander who had been recommended by the Community Board (of which I was vice chairman, and an active participant) for promotion to deputy inspector. And he was! We recommended him for this promotion, with the proviso that he not be transferred from the precinct, because he had cooperated with us during his tenure and gave us the impression that he considered us as partners in the effort to fight crime.

Following his first meeting with his superiors, after the election of the racist mayor of New York City, he came to our succeeding general meeting to announce that he had instructed his men to engage in a new, "in your face" approach to crime-fighting. When this meeting had concluded, I invited him to our next executive board meeting at which time I, and others, took him to task on his utterances and reminded him that the "in your face" approach was confrontational and would cause more problems with the police than it would solve.

He apologized and "explained" that he meant no harm, that it was just a football term which expressed their resolve to be aggressive in fighting crime, but that he intended to continue to work cooperatively with the community. I do not know whether he kept his promise because I moved from the community soon afterward, and my understanding is that he left not long afterwards, when he was promoted to the rank of inspector, and the last I heard of him, he had been upgraded to chief.

He was one of the few examples of police persons who at least made an attempt to portray law enforcement as cooperative to communities, even if not impartial. The tempo of the relationship of police to the Black community is one of "search and destroy." This is evident in the many cases of police brutality and assassinations. In New York City, alone, we note just a few of the many atrocities:

The murder of Eleanor Bumpers occurred in the 1970s and involved New York's finest killers.

Mrs. Bumpers was an old Black lady whose home was invaded by undercover policemen. She was disoriented and, believing, rightfully, that she was at risk, she grabbed a knife to defend her home. One cop shot her hand off and, left without her hand and unable to be a threat to anyone, another cop proceeded to kill her in cold blood.

As is usual, her accusers were exonerated by the powers that be.

Abner Louima was at a party in Brooklyn, New York, which was raided by the police. An altercation ensued and he was accused of resisting arrest.

The "punishment" for "assaulting" Officer Volpe was that Volpe and his fellow officers took him into the precinct bathroom and pushed a plunger handle into his rectum, causing him almost fatal damage. It has taken Mr. Louima many years to be mostly physically recovered, but he will never fully recover from the psychological damage.

The usual arguments, about renegade cops, do not apply in this case. This cruelty occurred in the precinct. This could not have happened without the implicit or explicit support of the commander and his underlings. They would have been drummed out of the force and put in prison if the desk sergeant, the executive officer, and the commander, as well as others in the chain of command, up to the mayor, did not support them, in spite of what they may do. They also knew that if they are arrested, they would have the unconditional support of their union and would have only had to opt to go to trial before a lone judge, and they would be exonerated.

The assassination of Amadou Diallo was the single, most horrific crime committed by members of the New York City police department, prior to Sean Bell in 2006.

Four "plain clothes" policemen entered the vestibule of the apartment building where this innocent African immigrant resided, accosted him, accused him of "acting suspiciously" and fired forty-plus shots at him, including some into him after he had fallen and was already dead. They say that their lives were endangered. By an innocent, unarmed man, whose only crime was of being Black. They moved this trial to Albany, New York, because they said that they could not get a fair trial because there was too much "publicity." The truth is that they moved the trial because they got a Black judge in Bronx County who would, more than likely, have not exonerated them.

The "powers" rejoiced in that the jury that was eventually selected was "mixed" but that could work in the policemen's favor, because there needed to be a unanimous verdict to convict the killers. This normally means that a mixed jury might not find them guilty or innocent, resulting in a hung jury. If this happens, and a second trial has the same result, they might walk free. At any rate, as a prelude of what was to be expected, the prosecutor asked that the jury consider lesser charges, which might result in their being found guilty but not serving a single day in prison. That happened, and justice, once again, evaded the Black community.

And the legal brutality of our community also continues.

While leaving a nightclub, where he and his friends had just celebrated the end of his bachelor days, Sean Bell and two of his friends were gunned down in a hail of **fifty** bullets, by four policemen. In a scene that seems to have been orchestrated to outdo the Amadou Diallo debacle, these policemen shot these men as if they were crazed animals, and they were fighting for their lives. It is as if they were thinking, "We can outdo the Diallo group. We can kill the rabid dogs with more bullets." In fairness to two of the officers who, between them fired only about four shots, the blame must go, mostly, to the other two.

One mad dog fired thirty-odd shots, and reloading in the process. Are these people human? How can one shoot another human being so many times? How many shots does it take to kill a Black man? *Or, maybe it's because they can't shoot straight why they have to fire so many times!* Whatever it is, it is just another example of the low esteem that the police have for people in the so-called minority communities, especially Blacks.

As usual, the Detective Union supported the officers, unconditionally. The police even sought to "criminalize" Bell, as if to say he deserved it because he is a criminal or to have him lose the sympathy of the community. They even "found" their mystery witness who sought to show that they were justified. It is never justified to shoot fifty bullets at someone who is not shooting back!

So, parents are left grieving, once again. Brothers and sisters, and grandparents, and aunts and uncles, and children, and cousins, and friends, are once again bereaved and outraged. And hatred builds some more, and the communities are further splintered. And injustice continues to prevail. And we continue to ask why. Why do they kill us? Why do they frame us and send us to prisons, when we're innocent? Why do they seek to destroy our community and try to annihilate us, as they do our history? Are they so insecure, or is hatred their motive? They continue to treat us as slaves, with our only duty to serve the master and, if we won't do it in jail, then we should be eliminated.

Why else would they kill the Sean Bells, and the Diallos, and the Jamals, and the Muhammads, and the Sekous and the Jóses, and..., and.... Still they continue in 2010. On April 25, 2010 *one more* atrocity was added. A young Black attorney was one of the witnesses as a Black man was shot to death by Culver City, California, police officer while the victim had his hands high and his fingers spread. When she confronted them on this butchery, they claimed he had a weapon in his car. She had to remind them that he was away from the car and was not a threat. Luckily, she was there!

One more . . . and counting. When will we become strong enough to stop it?

And the city, and the state, and the nation, and the world look on! And people who scream their civility look on! And the silent majority is silent! They are secretly happy about these events? They are locked in their castles and they and their families are protected by these same denizens of doom to the "minorities" of the world. They will not complain because their estates are secured and the "undesirables" are being eradicated *en masse.*

Evil exists and multiplies because good people do nothing. But where are the good people?

If this holocaust is not halted by the authorities, then we must be the ones to halt them. Take control of our lives and make the murderers pay!!!

The Koven of Klansmen Kops. Policemen must come from the community where they serve. The reason is that the police must have a vested interest in the community in order to really have its interest at heart. If not, the community is in deep trouble. This fact is confirmed by a case of Ku Klux Klan infiltration of the police departments.

In 1998 many policemen were investigated and most dismissed for their involvement in a Klan retreat in the hills of Tennessee. And to accentuate the severity of the situation, there was a large percentage of high-ranking police officials involved.

It is not enough to hire persons for the police force (after intense scrutiny and psychological evaluations), but they must be monitored throughout their careers. How one thinks influences all aspects of one's behavior, so one cannot expect racists to act fairly toward people they despise. Although everyone knows that there is absolutely no one without bias, we must be sure that law-enforcement people at all levels have a sense of justice within them.

The fact that there were so many police persons involved in this coven and that this group represents a very small percentage of the law enforcement persons with racist views, should be of grave concern to all decent, law-abiding people, of whatever race. These people must be eliminated from law enforcement.

How can we expect that innocent, non-White people will not continue to be framed, or that White law breakers will be disciplined, equally, if we allow these criminals to continue to carry badges. Reference the case of the undercover detective in Tulia, Texas (*discussed elsewhere*), or the "Raid at Goose Creek" (*also discussed elsewhere*), as two examples in the millions of serious abuse of power by racist law-enforcement personnel. The average Black person is able to recount many personal incidents of police abuse and brutality.

So we need our own police. This will not totally eliminate abuse, but it will be guaranteed to reduce it by ninety-nine percent.

The (In)justice System

The laws of this country have always favored the caucasian members of the population. What's more, it specifically favors the elite of this class, with descending levels of favor as one gets darker and/or poorer, as the case may be.

There have been many instances of this discrepancy over the years. One has only to look from the popularity of the "Jim Crow" statutes to the Dred Scott edict to the O. J. Simpson fiasco, and to the present and continuing cases of misapplication of the justice system to the benefit of one group and the detriment of other groups.

I am particularly concerned about some cases, which had been in the news in mid-July of 1998. There was the continuing saga of the Crown Heights, Brooklyn, "riot" where a Black man who is alleged to have said, "kill the Jews" has been sentenced to serve twenty-one years in prison. According to the judge, he would have received a shorter sentence, but he was not penitent. Compare this with the sentence of the two White youngsters who admittedly slaughtered their newborn child in

Delaware, and who received two years and two-and-a-half years in prison, respectively.

Look at the case of the teenager who gave birth in the bathroom at the locale of her prom, disposed of the baby, and returned to partying. She, also, pleaded guilty and received a slap on the wrist.

Then there is the case of a retarded Florida boy who, while imitating the wrestling moves he saw on TV, strangled a five-year-old little girl, and she died. Even though he did not understand the implications of what he was doing and the resulting tragedy, he was sentenced to twenty-five years to life, in prison. Public outcry has since caused a reversal, but he spent a couple of years in prison.

It is not hard to figure out which "perpetrators" are Black. The results speak volumes.

Then let us examine the case in Poughkeepsie, New York, of a White, former assistant district attorney who was implicated in the rape of a then 15-year-old Black girl. The evidence showed that, prior to being named as a co-defendant, he went to the doctor for treatment for stress-related symptoms. Furthermore, one of the alleged co-defendants committed suicide, and others alibied one another in the absence of any independent alibi. The advisors rightfully pointed the finger at the accused and demanded justice. They forgot, however, that they were dealing with folks in "up south" New York.

A “grand jury” found the accused DA innocent of all charges and said that the victim had lied about being raped, etc. Now, I’ve never heard of a grand jury assessing innocence. My knowledge is that a grand jury decides whether there is sufficient evidence to indict a person. To my knowledge, the victim did not appear before the grand jury, so they could conclude only that there was not enough evidence “provided” to indict.

Ten years later, the accused ADA decided to sue the Black advisors. Why ten years later? It is my understanding that the statute of limitation on the rape charge had expired and so, even if the former accused was now further implicated or evidence found of his culpability, he could not be prosecuted. If that is the case, his culpability seems all the more apparent.

Not surprisingly, a jury “of his peers” found that he had been libeled and slandered and awarded him damages.

Let’s review: A White man is accused of raping a Black girl. He is an assistant district attorney in a small, predominantly White town, controlled by his friends and family. His father is reputed to be a judge, and a colleague of the judge(s) who arbitrated the “cases.” Does one think that there is more than a one-percent chance that he would go to trial and be convicted, even if he is guilty?

The case of O. J. Simpson is one that has caused very heated discussions and arguments for a number of years and will continue to do so. I will, therefore, start out by saying that I will not try to find the answer to who killed Nicole Simpson or Ron Goldman, but will only postulate a few ideas concerning the case.

Why was his Bronco parked outside the compound when he had more than enough space inside the gated property for the vehicle, especially when that condition was necessary to legally allow the police to enter the compound? If a person had just killed two persons, severing the aorta of at least one of them, there would be a profusion of blood that would, literally, ooze off the killer's clothes and person.

How could there be only a couple tiny drops of blood inside and outside the vehicle the person drove while attired in these clothes? If this same person goes into a house and travels upstairs in these clothes (or at least some of it), how can there be only one or two tiny drops of blood on white carpeting. And what happened to the missing vial of blood that was extracted from O. J., which couldn't be found at the lab? Could this not be the source of these droplets?

So O. J. was smart enough to wear gloves to disguise his fingerprints and a mask to disguise his features. How come he was dumb enough to take the gloves and throw them inside his own premises where all suspicion would be on him? So what happened why the gloves were not cut and there was no blood inside of it, even though O. J. was supposed to have had his finger cut while committing this dastardly act of murder? How come he traveled to Chicago on an aeroplane, signed autographs and chatted with passengers and crew and no one saw a laceration on his hands or fingers? Yet his laceration was fully noticed on his way back from Chicago. Is it implausible that an ex-wife or an ex-husband could be so affected by the cruel murder of that former spouse to injure him- or herself from the shock? I would say not!

Are we to assume that one person killed both of these victims? We know that Simpson was a strong ex-football star, but what was one victim doing while he was killing the second? We are told that the evidence shows that the victims put up a fight. Silently? Wouldn't a single perpetrator be injured? After all, Goldman was athletic, and I'm sure that Nicole would not have stood back and watch him get killed without taking some action. Nor would he be immobile.

The evidence points to more than one killer, and my belief is that Cato knows who they are, even if he might not have participated. He had opportunity, if not motive, which he may also have. He is reported to have had keys to the Bronco and the mansion, as well as to Nicole's home. He might have been in cahoots with that racist cop. Or he might be quiet to save his own life?

Nicole might have been killed because she was involved in drugs, or because she had been in a relationship with a "nigger," by the aforementioned cop and his cronies. She might have been killed by drug persons, with whom she is reputed to have been involved. In either of those scenarios, Goldman was just in the wrong place at the wrong time.

It could also be that he was the target. There are rumors that he owed money to the "wrong people" and he was eliminated for that. In which case Nicole was in the wrong place at the wrong time.

Only the killers and the victims know, for sure, what occurred. The rest of us are only speculating, and we have many and varied feelings about the "butcherings".

In spite of O. J.'s book, *If I Did It*, which should have been published in November, 2006, and people's belief that it confirmed his involvement, this author still holds to the belief that he was innocent. What I think happened is that he has been used to living a certain lifestyle which he could not now afford and that someone planted the idea in his head that writing such a book would make him some money. It did, in spite of the fact that the book has been withdrawn from publication.

However, our concern here is the racial underpinnings surrounding this case. It split America along racial lines, for the most part. The vast majority of Whites think that Simpson is the killer, notwithstanding the evidence (or lack of it). The vast majority of Blacks think that he is innocent. The others have honed their thoughts on the matter from the news media which is White controlled and which slants almost everything to fit the image which the majority White population wishes to portray. According to their gospel, if you are Black you are a criminal, or you have the propensity to be one. If you are White, you are automatically a good, decent person, with very few exceptions. But that is not true.

The powers-that-be followed and harassed O.J. for many years and arrested him many "crimes" which they could not make stick. They finally "nailed" O.J. in 2008, for attempting to recover his stolen memorabilia (with the use of a gun?). Now they finally have him in prison. He should have expected that they would stop at nothing to get him, but he could not be cured of his "jungle fever."

The court system is organized to protect the rich and powerful and to keep the poor people "in their places." All one has to do to verify this statement is to look at how the injustice is administered. If one is poor one catches hell, and if one is black hell catches one. There are undoubtedly tens of thousands of innocent Black people in prison and tens of thousands of guilty Whites walking free.

If a Black person is convicted of any crime the powers that be make sure that everything he has is taken away and he becomes poverty-stricken. To begin with, bail is set at a high limit and fines are heartlessly exorbitant. Compare this with the bail for the average White perpetrator. Many are released in their own recognizance or to relatives. They aren't stripped of all worldly possessions.

When one looks at the societal ills and the way the society (and the criminal (in)justice system) treat people of color, it is a wonder that we don't all go mad and kill all the White people, as well as ourselves. The fact that we don't do that is a testament of our strength and our morality.

The Prison-Industrial System

The prison-industrial system in the United States is a huge conglomerate. It is a multi-billion-dollar industry, which has a great impact on the American economy and way of life.

Dr. Milfred Fierce, of Brooklyn College in New York, wrote a scalding book on the atrocities of the powers-that-be in supplying clients to that system post-"emancipation." According to Dr. Fierce's research, newly "freed" African Americans were routinely rounded up, arrested on trumped-up charges and incarcerated. Their services were then sold to manufacturers and other business entities for whom they produced goods and services at "slave" labor prices.

Currently, the same thing is being done to Black people in these United States and, as noted elsewhere, whole communities are built on the support of the prison system. If significantly fewer Black and Latino people are sent to prison, whole towns will become abandoned wastelands. And that will not be allowed to happen!

We cannot be surprised, then, that we and our children are being harassed by the police because, when we get angry and answer or strike back we can be charged with disturbing the peace and resisting arrest, at the very least. If we observe the police acting in an inhumane manner and comment, or even critically watch the abuse, we can be charged with obstruction of justice. We are also in danger of being attacked by the police, or shot down in cold blood if they "feel threatened" by our action or non-action. African American and Latino peoples are an endangered species in America!

The prison system is also a training ground for true criminal activity. It is a university where petty criminals learn the art of crime from the "professsors." It is a place where crime is allowed to flourish and where both men and women are raped by both inmates and guards. It is a place where hopelessness and helplessness abound, where people know they will return, but there is nothing that they can do about it because, once they enter that system, they will be targeted by "law enforcement agencies" every time a crime is committed, by any-one. Furthermore, they will lose their "privileges" as citizens, and become unemployable. These, and other factors, contribute to the high recidivism rate and guarantee workers for the system.

So, even though we can't win the war to protect ourselves, and our children, in the short run, we must work hard to win some of the battles. By paying close attention to our offspring and steering them away from the path of the law-enforcement personnel, including the police and the court system, which is part and parcel of the problem!

If we do that, we will have a chance to keep most of our people from the shackles of the racist, oppressive system.

Review

How do we "overcome" some of the political pitfalls to the Black community? What must we do to have proper representation with respect to our elected officials, police and fire protection, or any other governmental service for which *we pay*, whether literally or figuratively? We must learn the rules and force changes wherever necessary. Here are a few guidelines:

1. Learn how the political system works.

2. Educate our children, and others, about the process.

3. Select the candidates, carefully, looking at short-term and long-term effects on the locality and the nation. For example, electing a likeable (or even competent) person to an office will strengthen or facilitate a party's hold on an office, which may bring negative results. Even though the individual may be hard-working and honest, his/her election may help a party fulfill a negative agenda, because it gives it the numbers to operate a government.

4. If the elected person is not sensitive to the needs of the community, or does not work for the needs of the community, don't be afraid to fire him/her with your nay vote at the next election.

5. Look at the party's platform. That is more important than the individual's ideas, by far. The politician operates by the party's thoughts and actions. The individual needs support from colleagues in order to pass legislation, ratify a budget, or to take almost any action, large or small. It cannot be done by any individual, alone, no matter how altruistic that individual may be! So, vote for the party ideals you believe in, and then your favorite candidate within that party group.

6. Be very careful in looking at the history of the individual *and* the party. There are many newly converted politicians, who sway with the wind and will be whatever we want them to be.

They'll tell us how they believe in equality and civil rights and how the other party is taking us for granted. You must evaluate whether the party is just seeking to win or maintain power or whether they traditionally included Black folks.

7. Most importantly, we must be universal in our expectations from a party or a candidate. We should never seek individual benefits but, instead, seek benefits which are most important to us all, as a whole. Remember, as goes the least of us, so goes the rest of us. Many people think that if a politician "brings" a senior center to his/her district, that person is "the bomb" and should be re-elected. That is not necessarily so. The methods and opportunity costs are also important. Look at whether two other Black districts were "sold out" in order for this person to have this accomplishment. It is okay to say "Go to hell" to a briber and lose that largesse, if you are doing it as part of a unity stand. Together, more will be had for all the people. That must be the stance and there should be no wavering.

We must use the newly-found potential political strength in a united, concerted way to advance our well-being. What is the use of fighting and dying for equality if we do not insist on it, and use whatever clout we have to make it work for us?

We have potential political strength but we must learn how to leverage it to the benefit of ourselves, and our community.

Section V

Economic Activities

The economist Karl Marx (and others) spoke of the fall of the capitalist economic system. They were right. It will eventually fall. Of course, his socialist system is also not feasible, as he seems to have come to realize in his later life. One has only to look at the former Soviet Union and its economic corruption, which helped lead to its downfall.

The capitalist system is a constant war of the ownership versus the workers, with the owners winning, in the short term but, in the long term, it will be *zero sum*. There will be no winners!

The economic struggle affects us all, and Blacks must remain ever vigilant of its ramifications. Consider the fact that we remain at the bottom of the economic ladder so that if the ladder falls, we will be completely crushed. We should be concerned because the once mighty dollar is almost useless, and it is becoming more so each day.

The author was once involved in a discussion with a number of businesspersons at a "power breakfast" and was nearly "lynched" for daring to say that Black people were worst off in 2002 than we were in 1965. It was, first of all, very difficult to get anyone to listen to the facts about the value of the 2002 dollar in relation to the 1965 dollar. Furthermore, there is the fact that Blacks had lost ownership of many valuable commodities (land, businesses, control of our schools and community organizations, etc.). One particular gentleman suggested that I go investigate the new opportunities open to us, and the one hundred thousand dollars-a-year salaries which some of us were now earning.

While his argument was correct about the salaries, he missed the whole point. He "could not see the forest for the trees." Worth cannot be measured in numbers of dollars alone. The value of that dollar is important. What can that dollar buy today, compared to its 1965 clout?

In 1965, when this author had his first job, the salary was $100.00 per week. Total taxes was $17.00+, leaving a disposable income of $82.00-plus per week. Forty dollars were deposited into a savings account (40%); fifteen dollars were contributed for food and lodging (the rent for the five-room apartment was $55.00 per month); transportation to and from work was $2.00 weekly; and the rest was spent on food, clothes, entertainment, and the like. There was usually some left over to put into the savings account. And there was no attempt to "skimp!"

Compare that dollar-power with 2002. Two thousand dollars per week (or approximately

$100,000.00 per year, which is twenty-fold the above-mentioned 1965 income) would not have the same power. From one hundred thousand dollars, the taxes would devour about 40%-45%. One would be lucky to be able to save 10% because that same apartment now rented for about $1,500.00+ per month; the carfare was now $20.00+ per week; and the cost of food, clothes, and entertainment were increased about fifteen-fold. The result is that more people in this country were "borderline", economically, and Black people were more and more poverty-stricken and homeless.

Now let's get back to the capitalist system for awhile. As previously stated, it is in deep trouble, for a number of reasons. The most important is the constant (and accelerated) shift of wealth from the poor to the rich and the damming up of the loopholes which, heretofore, enabled a few people to be able to pull themselves up "by the bootstraps."

The system is locked in a battle, which tolls its death knell, and the protagonists do not seem to understand what is happening. The capitalist system is, supposedly, based on the "market economy." This means that the demands of the market (need for goods and services) control production and cost. It assumes that consumers have a choice to demand or not demand the goods. This seems all well and good in theory, but there are certain things that are necessities which people must have regardless of the cost. These include food, shelter and clothing, among others. Take, for example, the price of oil. Oil is a limited resource that, in itself, inflates the price.

However, notwithstanding a slight downward trend in price with a dip in demand, the price of oil remains high because it is a necessary resource for most means of production and for heating and cooling.

Another great threat to the capitalist system is the labor-management relationship. In their 2005 negotiations with the City of New York and the Transit Authority, respectively, the United Federation of Teachers and the Transit Union both cited the fact that management was in a "surplus" fiscal situation, so they should be given larger raises.

In theory, one cannot argue with their logic. However, in order to have those surpluses, both the City and the Transit Authority have had to increase its taxes and its fares, respectively. If they increase wages and benefits, they will have to run the risk of another deficit and will have to go back to their constituencies for more money, thereby triggering further inflation. This, in turn, will devalue the buying power of the raises which the workers received (remember that they are part of the constituencies) and place them in need of further cost-of-living adjustments, etc., etc.

But why should Black people be concerned about the foregoing? To repeat, because we are at the bottom rung of the economic ladder and so, every change in the economic system affects us doubly negatively. So we must be ever vigilant to not only guard ourselves from economic destruction, but we must endeavor to improve our lot and move from the "cellar."

In order to do that, we must understand our current position, identify where we want to go, learn the system, map our course, start the journey, not be dissuaded by the rough road, arrive at our destination, stake our claim, and protect our territory.

An April 5, 2001, article by Dan Harris on ABC.com, tells the story of an ad placed in college newspapers by a David Horowitz, entitled "Ten Reasons Why Reparations for Blacks is a Bad Idea for Blacks—And Racist, Too." He claims "Blacks owe a debt to the United States for the freedom and economic benefits they've enjoyed since the Civil War." He adds, "A hundred years later, Black Americans are the tenth richest nation in the world. That is a remarkable success story that no one wants to talk about." Yes! But what is the percentage of the Black population and what is the Black wealth compared to the GNP? We are more than ten percent of the population with less than one percent of the wealth. So Mr. Horowitz can fool no one who is intelligent. Furthermore, the Black slaves built the early economy of the U.S. and, therefore, the foundation for this nation's wealth. How much did Mr. Horowitz's fore-parents contribute? And what does he think of the Jewish reparations from Germany and Switzerland?

On the ABC program, "60 Minutes," the remarkable champion for reparations to the African American descendants of former slaves, was interviewed, along with other "voices" on the subject. I will not give notoriety to some of the interviewees by identifying them, but some of the "colored" people interviewed were remarkable in their stupidity regarding the subject. One person praised the U.S.A. for providing great opportunities for Blacks and compared the lifestyles and freedoms of these people to those on the African continent, and elsewhere.

They make no allowance for the resulting devastation to Africa by the theft of 50 million people from Africa during the slave trade, with the result of tremendous brain-drain from the continent. These same people used these brains and brawn to help build the Americas.

There is no business or enterprise in which a black person is involved from which a white person does not derive some benefit! They benefit when we are born, while we are alive, and when we die. The reverse, certainly, is not the case.

Therefore, Whites should not be so set on preventing people of color from operating our own enterprises. Or should they? Is it not about buying fish versus learning to fish? Notwithstanding the resistance, it is imperative that we do learn to fish, so to speak, because that is the only way we can guarantee the means of feeding our families.

This fact was "brought home" to this author during the 1993 Crown Heights incident in Brooklyn, New York, when a Jewish man made the statement that if the Blacks insisted on attacking Jews, then the Jews should "fire" the whole lot of them from their jobs. The implications are that the Blacks are dependent on the Jews for their livelihood and means of subsistence. And that is, to a great extent, gospel.

The chains must be broken! We must seize our destiny!

There is a story repeated by the authors of *Think and Grow Rich*, as retold by Russell H. Conwell (probably quoted from *The Secret of the Ages*). This story is worth repeating over and over again. It is about an African farmer who settled on barren, rocky land, and who grew tired of an inability to reap profitable crops. So he decided to abandon his venture and seek his riches as others did, searching for diamonds. While he was so occupied, however, the man who had bought his property discovered a rock, which proved to be one of the largest diamonds ever found and this land turned out to contain one of the largest deposits of diamond ore. The moral of the story, as they concluded, is that the first farmer did not spend the time—once he decided to hunt for diamonds—to find out what they looked like in the rough, or he would have discovered his riches right there. Instead, he continued to search for the elusive diamonds, and died in poverty.

We African Americans are not only surrounded by wealth, but it passes through our hands everyday. The problem is that we are too busy looking at who is keeping it from us so we cannot see the way to harness it. Here is a guidepost.

Presently, only approximately two to four percent of the disposable income of African Americans is spent within our own community. This compares unfavorably with other ethnic groups, where more than half of their disposable income is spent within their own communities. In the Jewish community, for example, more than ninety percent is retained.

Disposable Income and Its Importance to a Community

Disposable income is that amount of one's paycheck, or other source of revenue, which one retains after all taxes have been paid. In other words, it is the money which one has for oneself and which one can decide how to spend.

For most people, their disposable income is all the money they control, and so it is critical that they begin to make the right spending decisions, with an eye toward enriching themselves and their community by those decisions.

Presently, in the African American community, one will see a predominance of people of other ethnic groups controlling the businesses and other enterprises, while listening to the residents complain about the lack of wealth in their neck of the woods.

It is interesting to note, however, that the noisiest complainants are those who refuse to spend their money with people who look like them and who live in the neighborhood. The fact is that the circulation of the disposable income within a community has immeasurable benefits. Its impact on a community has geometric proportions.

Consider what happens when a person decides to start a business within a community and is patronized by that community. First of all, the person becomes a role model not only to other adults (who might now see the possibility of their own success), but also to youngsters who might not have any other role models, or who might just want to become like that person, stay in school and work toward becoming an entrepreneur.

Secondly, as a business grows, one needs additional employees. The natural thing is for one to hire from the neighborhood, as opposed to seeking such help from outside. Therefore, unemployment will be reduced in that area, however much.

The third consideration, and an offshoot of the second, is that crime will be reduced, because many people commit crimes, such as shoplifting, burglary, and the like, because they need to feed themselves and/or their families, and they have no job and no hope. This situation is modified by that employment and also means that this parent or significant other is now a positive rather than a negative influence on his or her charges.

A fourth benefit is that the profits of the business are deposited in a neighborhood banking institution. The result is that this bank is now more financially solidified and can be better able to lend money not only to the business, but to other neighborhood residents for purchasing or "rehabilitating" property, paying tuition for college and other students, buying cars or other useful items.

The business person also has to pay taxes which is then used to improve the infrastructure and give better service to the residents, including the building of better educational institutions, day care centers, senior citizen centers, and the like.

A sixth, and very important benefit, is that the businessperson who is successful develops the financial clout to be able to demand better prices from his or her suppliers, some of which can be passed on to the consumer. It is important that most African Americans, when asked why they do not support businesses run by people of their same genre, will reply that the prices are too high, the quality is not as good, or that the service stinks.

The reality is that the prices are higher to African American businesspersons, partly because of racism, but also partly because they are not big enough and, as a result, do not have the clout to demand better prices. The quality, admittedly, in some cases might not be as good but some other factors come into play. The merchandise in a typical neighborhood store stays on the shelf a lot longer because of fewer customers. In the case of consumables, the loss is often tremendous.

It is also true that the workers in many community business places do not make the effort to be courteous and helpful but, in most other stores, African Americans are treated with the same or greater disrespect. Yet they smilingly patronize those persons, and seem to consider it an honor to be disrespected. There is never an excuse for rudeness or discourtesy, and so one should punish whomever treats them in this way by not patronizing them. One should not, however, seek petty excuses not to support one's own, as is now done in the African American community.

Control of Money

As there are varying estimates of the amount of disposable income in the African American community, so too is the estimate of the amount of money which is controlled by the group. One can postulate, however, that a good estimate is ten times the disposable income.

There are large numbers of African Americans who control budgets or who influence the budget decisions of many entities. If one starts with the churches, it is easy to see that they have large budgets. If we conclude that at least half of the members pay their ten-percent tithes and then their offerings and we multiply the amount by the number of members, that becomes a formidable sum. And we must not forget the amount given by members for special projects. As an example, the National Baptist Convention reportedly has over six million members. In addition to the contributions of members, many churches get government and private grants for special programs, and have schools and day care and/or senior care centers with fee-paying clients.

There are Black colleges and universities that have very large budgets and large contributions from their alumni and other sources, as well as other private schools with budgets.

As of 2010, there are many politicians who vote on expenditures at all levels of government and who influence where the billions of dollars are expended. For example, the former comptroller of the state of New York "controlled" a $50-billion-plus budget with a huge pension fund. While he did not make overall budget decisions, it was he who mostly decided where this pension fund was invested, as well as helping to decide who some of the vendors for state contracts should be. There are many Blacks within the New York City Department of Education who have control of large chunks of a budget of more than twenty billion dollars. The Mayors of the Cities of Atlanta and San Francisco, and dozens of other cities have large budgets that they influence. As do the governors of New York and Massachusetts.

Aside from the fact that many people of African extraction own small and medium sized businesses, there are thousands who have decision-making positions in small, medium and large corporations.

All of these people need to be sensitized to the knowledge that their community needs them to make a conscious decision to invest some of the capital which they control within their community, without regard to whomever wish to label them as reverse discriminators. At the very least, some of these persons must include Black brokers in their investment decisions.

The bottom line is that if each (or most) person decides to spend ten percent of the money that they control within the Black community, the net result is that it would equal to about the same as the total of disposable income. Imagine the impact! Instead of two to four percent of disposable being spent in the community, it would amount to the equivalent of one hundred percent of disposable. This would be a twenty-five to fifty-fold increase in the money that would be otherwise spent there and would have a mind-boggling positive effect.

Supposing, then, that this scenario was to ensue? Supposing half of that impact was realized? The bottom line is that there would be the aforementioned reduction in crime; hopelessness in the community would be almost eliminated; the twenty-odd percent adult unemployment, as well as the forty-odd percent youth unemployment would be below five and ten percent, respectively. All the other positive effects would also ensue, and the community would become almost self-sufficient.

It is to be remembered that, although Black Americans rue our lot, the disposable income of this group is far greater than the GNP of most nations. The problem is that we have not learned how to harness it to our benefit.

Let's postulate further on the above scenario where ten percent of the controlled funds are spent in the community. Imagine what would happen when an African American businessperson is doing well, because of increased clientele. That person can now demand of the supplier that better prices be given. Some of these savings could now be passed on to the consumer who would be more inclined to spend a larger than ten-percent portion of that expenditure with that businessperson.

The further result is that the "middle-man" can be eliminated, altogether, and the manufacturer can be accessed, directly. As a matter of fact, there will come a point where there will be enough financial incentive for these people to themselves engage in manufacturing and controlling their businesses at all levels.

There may be some who want to interpret this whole admonition and encouragement to African Americans as an attempt to sway them into buying only from other African Americans. The reply is that that conclusion is a lot of hogwash.

There will never be a time when any group will become totally self-sufficient in America. The groups have a symbiotic relationship. If one gets burnt, the others feel the pain, also. The message is that African Americans cannot sit back and wait to be given a "piece of the pie" or even the crumbs, for that matter, because nobody will give up what they have to another, especially not to someone he or she perceives as less deserving.

Gaining Financial Strength

It is amazing to know just how much potential there is in the African American community. One has only to look at the tremendous contributions this group has made to America throughout its history—and under some dire conditions. Most of the early inventions that have been patented to White slave masters have, in fact, been the work of slaves. However, since the law was that the property of property (the slaves) belonged to the master, the true inventors were not credited. This was seemingly the same for freed men as it was for slaves.

The following two examples speak volumes about the topic: Eli Whitney is credited with the invention of the cotton gin, but he had nothing to do with its "invention." What he did was to take a crude model made by a slave on his relatives' plantation in the South and had it mechanized in his northern hometown. He never invented a thing! (Since "necessity is the mother of invention", it is those who need to lighten their loads who invent the most.) Thomas Edison, on the other hand, patented the light bulb in his name, although the filament, without which it couldn't work, was really invented by Lewis Howard Latimer. The fact that Latimer sued Edison over this infringement three times and won the cases, did not convince anyone to change the history books to the truth. It was this same Latimer who made the model of the telephone which Alexander Graham Bell invented.

African Americans must begin to profit from the inventions that they create. This is not now the case. Most people who "create" are employed by corporations, which register the inventions in their own names. The problem is that the people who have ideas do not usually have the financial wherewithal to build and promote their inventions, thus the profits go to the folks "with the dough."

African Americans, in particular, as well as Africans on the continent and in the diaspora need to learn that any job situation is a learning opportunity to branch out on their own. They should be astute and alert learners who do their very best in their job environment with a number of things in mind: Firstly, if they do not perform, their employer's business may not succeed and they may not have jobs. Secondly, in order to guarantee increases in salary, the business needs to be profitable. They can then point to their contribution to the profitability in demanding raises. The third, and most important consideration, is that they are serving their apprenticeship in order to become "tradesmen" in their own endeavors, bearing in mind that practice makes perfect. The good habits they pick up while working for someone else carries over to their own. So do the bad habits. In the book, *Think and Grow Rich: A Black Choice,* Dennis

Kimbro points out that, regardless of for whom we work, we are all presidents of our own corporation, and are responsible for the assets we accumulate and the benefits which we accrue. So we should always aspire to use all our experiences for our own personal growth.

While it is true that everyone is not equipped to be businesspersons, there are some "closet" entrepreneurs. They have the potential, but this potential is never exploited. These individuals are fearful of the unknown, as most people are, and so they play it safe in a corporate setting.

There are others who get "tired of working for the man" and figure that they can start a business on their own. They go into business in their trade area without preparation or they look to see what "brother" seems to be making money and start the same type of business. Pretty soon they are out of business. Sometimes they even force the "brother" out of business, too, because of their competition in a "soft" market. This person can be called the hit-or-miss businessman.

The best examples of the hit-or-miss businessman can be found in the laundromat business or in the new book-selling area. It is not unusual to see one laundromat in an area seeming to do well. Very shortly, a second one appears on the next corner and some of the populace treks to the new guy. Not long afterward, a third "entrepreneur" appears with his "laundromat" on another corner, and soon the "closed" sign appears on one building, then another. Most times the original business survives, but sometimes all three will fail.

The same type of thing occurs in the bookselling business. There are dozens of people who have seen that a few people have started bookstores and small publishing businesses and have determined that they, too, can benefit from the "tremendous market potential." Some decide to sell on the street (sometimes very close to where a bookstore is located) and others decide to open stores. Some of them cannot even read, but what they do is to force the people with "overhead" out of business. Some churches and schools have also jumped on the misdirected bandwagon to further *nail the coffin of these entrepreneurs shut.*

It is important to know that not every tradesman can become a good businessman, nor *vice versa.* The caveat is true, however, that if one wants to succeed, one has to prepare for success. It is not enough to know one's trade. One must also spend the time to learn the rudiments of business if one is to succeed. Find a training center or college or other relevant institution or do an "apprenticeship" in the business area.

There are many things to consider when starting a business. How will it be financed? Who are the clients? Where will the business be located?

Will this business fill a need or create a glut? Are workers available in the locale? What sort of business structure will be created, and why? Should the business be started from "scratch" or should an ongoing business be purchased?

The adage that it takes money to make money is gospel. The reason most people are poor is because they are poor. This might seem like double talk, but if one believes that it's not so, try to get a loan for a poor person. A bank wants to know that it will be repaid before issuing a loan. After all, it is responsible to its stockholders for its profit (or loss) and so one has to "qualify" for such a loan. The wealthy person, for the most part, is qualified by means of already having wealth. Therefore, the wealthy person will be able to borrow additional funds to invest and increase his/her wealth.

Some Economic Beacons

There have been a number of African Americans who have managed, in spite of significant restrictions, to accumulate quite a "nest-egg." Some of them are as follows:

Frederick Douglass. Frederick Douglass was born into slavery, but slavery was not born in him, so he resisted it with all his being. He is described by *Africana* encyclopedia as "the principal nineteenth-century African American spokesperson, reformer, abolitionist, author and orator.

Frederick Douglass was an abolitionist who traveled the U.S. and Europe speaking of the evils of slavery and the hypocrisy of the Americans who advocated the doctrine of all men being created equal with an inalienable right to life, liberty and the pursuit of happiness. He noted that while they spouted the words of liberty, they had the Negro in chains and treated him worse than they did their cattle. He refused to compromise his beliefs and his resolve to see all his people free, and gathered a cadre of supporters who worked for the cause of manumission.

He managed, also, to attract funding for his cause and himself and seemed to have invested well because he is reputed to have lived "pretty well" in his final years.

Earl G. Graves. Earl G. Graves is a nationally recognized authority on Black businesses and the publisher of *Black Enterprise* magazine, of which he is president and CEO. Having worked for Robert F. Kennedy, Graves cashed in on his knowledge of Washington and his entrepreneurial spirit when he began his venture and the magazine enjoys worldwide acclaim.

What better way to make money than to help others to make it? This he has done. He is one of those pioneers who have had a dream and have been willing to have that dream fulfilled through their own hard work and belief in themselves, instead of cowering in the face of opposition, however stiff it is.

In addition to his magazine holdings, Graves is chairman and CEO of one of the largest Pepsi-Cola franchises in the United States, Pepsi-Cola of Washington and he serves on the boards of several of the largest American corporations. He is an example of what is possible when we act instead of complain.

Magic Johnson. Ervin (Magic) Johnson seems, of all the sports figures to have "made it", to be the most conscious and erudite investor. He has parleyed his fame and financial largesse into a multi-faceted business venture that includes a chain of movie theaters, condominiums, and other enterprises which benefit others, while bringing him significant wealth.

He has brought the same discipline, which he displayed as a basketball superstar (mostly with the Los Angeles Lakers), into the business world. He is seen as someone who is "level-headed" and sincere and he is a role-model who youngsters not only can, but should, emulate.

John H. Johnson. John H. Johnson was born in Mississippi of humble beginnings and, in 1945, he founded the Johnson Publishing Company with the publication of *The Negro Digest*. He later launched *Ebony* magazine and then *Jet*. Although he eventually had to discontinue the publication of *The Negro Digest* when circulation plummeted, the company expanded into book publishing and cosmetics. For many years John H. Johnson was the richest African American, with significant influence and esteem.

He gave voice to the African American causes and publicized injustices to, and successes by, the race, at a time when there was hardly any voice and he played an important and pivotal role in the improvement of the Black community.

Michael Jordan. Michael Jordan is considered to be the best all-round basketball player in the history of the game. As such, he had become the highest paid athlete in the world, with his Nike and myriad of other endorsements. He bought a partnership in a basketball team but had to relinquish that when he was pressed back into service to play for the team. He has made a myriad of other investments that has set him up for an easy financial time for the rest of his life.

Michael Jordan is a symbol of what people can do if they put their minds to it and work hard. The only down side to his fame is that all the young men "want to be like Mike" and, instead of concentrating on education and other important aspects of their lives, they all want to play basketball, even though they have limited talents in that area.

Reginald Lewis. Reginald Lewis was born to a Baltimore, Maryland, working-class family and had told his family that he would become a millionaire because, he reasoned, "Why should white guys have all the fun." He finished college and, without even submitting an application, he was admitted to Harvard Law School. Having received his law degree, he set up practice and faltered for a little while before deciding to become an investment attorney.

He became an investor, bought the McCall Pattern Company for $22.5 million (using junk bonds), built it to profitability in a short time, and sold it for $65 million. He later leveraged that sale into buying Beatrice Foods for over $950 million dollars. That was one of the greatest blockbuster deals of its time, and increased his net worth to approximately $400 million, making him the wealthiest African American up to that time.

Unfortunately, he died of brain hemorrhage at the age of 50 years old, so we will never know the limits to which he might have risen in the business world. He, however, left a legacy of perseverance and success for those of us who might be, at times, discouraged to look towards and pattern.

Madame C. J. Walker. Sarah Walker was the daughter of former slaves who rose from her situation of poverty to become the first known African American millionaire (at a time when becoming a millionaire was a significant accomplishment).

Her claim to fame is that she developed and marketed special hair care products and styling techniques for Black women at a time when no such products existed. She organized a door-to-door sales force, established a school to teach women how to use her products, and established a mail-order wing.

She married C. J. Walker, a newspaperman who, it is said, played a significant role in her business success, but they split over business method disagreements. She was dubbed Madame C. J. Walker. She contributed, financially, to Black women's education, among other causes, in the Black community and left an indelible imprint in her horizons.

Oprah Winfrey. Oprah Winfrey is the wealthiest African American in the United States in the year 2010. She did not become so because she is lucky (although one needs some luck to be in the right place at the right time), but because she has the ambition, she prepared herself well, took advantage of her opportunities with her can-do attitude, and leveraged one success into another. She also pays it forward by helping others along the way, and empowering them to further help others.

She is the consummate professional, who does not walk around with a chip on her shoulders, but believes that if it can be done she can do it. And she does. She recognizes herself as a Black woman and is proud of that fact, but does not waste time belaboring it. She is proud of who she is, from where she came and the improvement she has made to her life. She has succeeded (maybe beyond her wildest dreams), but the success has not gone to her head. She is not liked by some, but is adored by others, and it seems not to bother her one way or the other. She is an example of the person some of us can be, and all of us can aspire to be.

There are hundreds of other shining examples of Black people who have persevered and advanced economically, and whose examples are beacons for those who would abandon the feelings and actions of inferiority and pursue the opportunities that are available to those with the right vision. They should be an inspiration to us all, a battle cry to move forward and upward in the spirit of Marcus Garvey, and the others. We should never let anyone or anything discourage us, in any way.

A story I have read is that of the Cubans of Miami who, when they began to arrive in the United States, found the bank doors "slammed in their faces." They had no money, no collateral, and no longevity here, in terms of work experience. After many futile attempts to get cooperation from the bank executives, they met and formulated a plan of self-help. The result is that most of the Miami banks are now owned by Cubans.

Similar experiences are shared by Koreans and other immigrants. The Koreans have also formulated a plan of self-help. They have used the sou-sou method to accumulate funds, which is used to help each businessman. The process goes like this: Ten businessmen will get together and put up, let's say a thousand dollars each, per week. All this money is given to one person to buy inventory or other necessity to promote his business.

The next week a second person receives the bounty, and so on, and so forth. They also have the policy of buying together, in order to enlarge their volume and reduce their cost. This combined effort increases their clout. It is understood that they have workers who, after working a number of years and long hours, will be helped to start their own businesses. It is no wonder that there are Korean-owned green grocery and other types of businesses all over the United States, mostly in African American neighborhoods.

It is important to add that they rarely ever live in the communities where they make their money, nor do they spend their money there. This group is not being singled out. The same can be said of the Irish, Italians, Jews and others before them, and will be repeated by whomever succeeds the Koreans as the exploiters of African American capital.

Notwithstanding the above-stated reality, money can be gotten through loans. If one has a good job, a good credit history and a good business plan, money might be obtainable from a banking institution by direct or secured loan through several sources, including the government. One example of governmental loan is through the Small Business Administration of the Federal government.

The direct loan is given to only a few qualified people, because the budget is limited, but they guarantee quite a number of loans. The thing is that the entrepreneur must otherwise be qualified for the loan from a bank, in which case the government "underwrites" it, guaranteeing the bank that if the borrower is unable to meet the obligation, the government will be responsible for the payment. Then the SBA will go after the borrower to recover the funds. Money is also available from state and local governments to help start a business, to renovate, etc. One can always inquire of the proper authorities what the requirements are because money is not loaned for *all* types of businesses.

Some people save their own money over a period of years to start sole proprietorship businesses. This can be a very slow process, depending on that person's income or the amount of capital investment and reserves the initial operation requires. One can tap credit unions or obtain home equity loans in order to help their dreams of business ownership come true. The admonition is that if the business fails, then there might be nothing left to "fall back on."

Starting a partnership enterprise is another good way to go, especially if the partner has the same interests or similar skills, or is a complement to one's own ability. The combined funds will make start-up, as well as operation, easier. There is always a down side to every up, and the downside is that partners always have a different way of doing things, as well as the fact that one is responsible for all of a partner's actions and debts relevant to the business.

Money can be borrowed from family members and from friends. The saying that money costs friends and relatives is true. Because of that, it is imperative that one does not fall prey to the inclination to make verbal agreements. Everything should be in writing and should be strictly adhered to. All probabilities should be anticipated and covered, including rate of interest and what happens in case of the death or disability of any of the parties.

If the corporate structure is the choice, the stockholders will all be expected to ante up a prescribed amount of money for each share of stock. This is probably the best structure if one chooses not to have a sole proprietorship. The corporation is considered to be like a separate individual and stockholders are protected from liability, except for the amount of their stock investment, unless they are officers of the corporation and personally guarantee something, like a loan, or if they act in a criminal manner. The corporate structure is not the be-all and end-all, however, because corporations have monetary liability to the government, even if they are losing money, whereas a sole proprietorship or a partnership pays taxes, for the most part, only on profits.

It is important to the business success that the businessperson knows the trade/profession. If a person has experience as a shoe salesman he will need to have training before he can present himself as a computer expert. Likewise, if he is a computer expert, but does not know the rudiments of salesmanship, he "will be left holding the bag" when people make their buying decisions because he will not know how to "sell" them on his computers.

There are people who have worked "on the assembly line" in their professions. They might be bookkeepers who have done only "accounts receivable" or "accounts payable" but they try to promote themselves as bona fide bookkeepers. They soon find themselves frustrated and out of business, and can't figure out why. And most of them don't take advice from anyone!

The conclusion is that one does not need to know everything about everything, because that is impossible, but one needs to complement oneself with people who are skilled in the areas of their weakness, and be willing and able to utilize those people's skills.

Sometimes businesspersons, like others, fall into a pit because they are afraid to give someone else credit where credit is due or because they are afraid of having "their thunder" stolen. The bottom line is that a leader "looks" better and is more successful surrounded by people who are efficient, than with people who are incompetent.

Where one is not expert and does not have one on staff, one should not hesitate to use consultants. The use of consultants also has the added benefit that one is not paying a full-time staff person for a job skill that is not needed all of the time.

No business survives without having "qualified" workers. The qualifications vary, depending on the type of business, but some traits are universal and must be present if a business is to succeed.

A good worker is one who is part of "us" instead of "them." One of the major problems one sees daily is the lack of "inclusion" of people in their fields of endeavor. The we/them syndrome is championing the cause of lethargy and non-accomplishment.

If a worker is not part of the "us" then that worker is a liability rather than an asset. So one needs to shed the outsiders and reward the insiders if one hopes to have any modicum of success. Being part of the "us" allow workers to do a little more to help the business to become stable and profitable, knowing that benefits will accrue not only to the employer, but to them, as well. Being part of the "us" allows them to be more courteous and helpful to clients and to be more patient with their fellow employees, as well as with the clients.

Being part of the "us" dissuades them from wasting time, materials, and energy, which could be used to build a business. Being part of the "us" means that they will encourage their co-workers to help the business rather than to sow seeds of discontent and undermine the enterprise.

Being part of the "us" means that the workers will be proud of their association with the business and promote it every chance they get.

For most businesses, location is a critical criterion. For example, if one is engaged in manufacturing and there is no direct interaction with consumers then one is less likely to worry about location, except with respect to transferring in raw material and shipping out the finished goods. The concern for location, then, will be based on proximity to transportation systems. On the other hand, a retail or service organization has to be concerned about its proximity to the consumers.

McDonald's is one of the companies that does a stringent market research. One will note that probably none of its locations is unprofitable. The reason is that it makes sure, before granting a franchise to anyone, that not only is that person properly trained, but that the proposed location is one where there is enough of a clientele to almost guarantee success. They are usually found in high-density business areas, along highways, or in poorer neighborhoods where people have a higher propensity to eat fast-food rather than cook, or where the single heads of household or the double wage earners are many times too tired to cook after a long day's toil. You will, conversely, mostly find businesspeople like Mercedes Benz or Lexus dealerships in, or close to, the "high rent" districts.

As suggested above, location and clientele go hand in hand. The clientele will determine your location. Some questions, which must be answered when determining the clientele, are:

(1) Is there a need for this product or service? (2) Where is the area of need? (3) Are there other similar businesses located in that area? (4) Are they capable of serving the whole community or is there room for another company, with growth potential for both? (5) If there is another business, is it serving the area properly and, are there many

complaints about it? (6) How strong is customer loyalty to that company? The answers to these questions will help you to determine whether you will locate there or choose another place.

Many persons start businesses that supply products or services that are not needed by the clientele they hope to attract.

One would not normally locate in a predominantly white area if one is selling black literature, nor would one attempt to sell pools in a poor black area. Aside from the poverty aspect, "blacks are *not buoyant enough?"* to be interested in swimming, according to a former Dodgers baseball team official. Of course, the real reason is that a pool is seen as a luxury, and Blacks don't, generally, have that kind of extra money to afford pools. The key to success is to find the need and to fill it. One should be cognizant, however, that as soon as others see him/her filling that need, they will get in to "share" the market.

The area of need will be the area which is either being under-served, or not served at all. One of the things that are "hot" now is the Internet. The result is that one is inundated with salespersons urging and cajoling one to "travel" to cyberspace. The reason that the Internet is so viable is that it is relatively new and exciting. No one wants to be left out when technology transforms the marketplace from a physical location where one travels to shop to a cyberspace address where one places orders to be shipped in a day or two. Those businesspersons who can directly benefit from this technology are well advised to get their sites secured.

To the question of whether other similar businesses are located in that area, the logical answer is in the question of whether a new enterprise will saturate the market and cause a downturn in the gross sales of the existing enterprises. Also, one needs to ask whether the existing enterprises are properly serving the clientele and whether this new business will be able to do a better job. If the answer is that one can do a better job or that the other companies do not have the interest of the community at heart, then one should go for it!

Customer loyalty is a critical consideration in determining whether to compete with a business entity. Some customers are loyal to a brand or a company, almost without justification at times. Some people will buy nothing but Levi jeans, even if other brands are better, nor will they purchase other than Nike sneakers or Japanese cars, even when conventional wisdom may be that those products are not cost effective.

In such situations, Joe's guaranteed top-of-the-line jeans, sneakers, or cars, at half the price, will still fail, because Joe's name means nothing to the consumer. The result is that Joe will be out of business if he competes head-to-head with these name brands, even though his products are of superior quality. If he hopes to remain in business he will have to target a different market than the ones his competitors have.

What about the work force? The work-force is determined by the type of product or skill being offered. If one is doing an ordinary, assembly-line type of business, then one would locate where the labor force is available, in abundance, and is fairly inexpensive. It would not hurt to locate in an area where there is high unemployment because it could provide jobs to competing workers. If one has a service business, such as computer programming and servicing, however, the first consideration is to attract highly skilled or easily trainable people, and one would select an area which would attract those professionals, as well.

Some years ago, in his television speech entitled *The Gospel According to Tony Brown,* Mr. Brown suggested that White people should fight racism and Black people should spend their time acquiring goods because that will get them the White "friends" which they seek.

What he fails to know is the following: as with anything else, White people, in general, will accept a few token Blacks who are well-off, but they feel threatened when they are confronted with many who are successful.

This is partly because it belies their claim of superiority and, partly because racism is not about black and white. It is about the green. So to ask White people to police themselves for the purpose of eradicating racism and allow us the opportunity to acquire a piece of the pie in the process is to ask the wolf to guard the sheep and protect them from harm.

Mr. Brown, notwithstanding his socio-political-cultural blindness, has tremendous economic insight. He has postulated, for a very long time, that it is the African American who is responsible for his/her own destiny. It is he/she who must become educated and economically astute and build his/her own future. It is he who, in recent times, admonished people in the community to not depend on others and to use the large fortunes which are expended, every day, to enrich white folks, to build for self. And everything he suggests can happen, economically, if his words are heeded!

Unfortunately, his political beliefs have clouded his mind, and he seems more interested in being the "one monkey" (*a la* W. E. B. DuBois), as well as leader of all. He spends too much time criticizing African American leaders—political and civic—while expounding his Republican doctrine. The fact is that the Republican "platform" is in opposition to not only people of color, but to all poor people. So how can a poor person be persuaded to make the enemy stronger by voting for him? The Republican Party is the party of the rich and, because Mr. Brown is rich, he is made to feel at home—especially since they can use him to point out what is wrong with Black people. This issue is further discussed in the section on Politics.

It is fair to say that as I have heard this gentleman speak on radio in succeeding months and years, I have begun to think that there is hope for his redemption. He has seemed to become emboldened in assessing blame and praise in a more objective manner and recognizing that the "saviors" have not come to save the Black folks, but that we must save ourselves. And, I might add, one another.

The Reparations Issue

The question of reparations for the families of African American slaves has been a topic of conversation for many, many years, predating Marcus Garvey and his back-to-Africa movement. In recent years this movement has been championed by Randall Robinson, as well as the late Queen Mother Moore, and a horde of other activists. Some of the questions most of us have are: Can it happen? Will it happen? If it does happen, what form will it take? How will it be administered?

Although there has been a vigorous resistance to the issue of reparations to Black Americans and

Native Americans, for many years—and at all levels—the payment of reparations for atrocities has had precedents. Not only has America paid reparations to Japanese Americans who were detained in encampments during World War II but, mostly on the instigation of America, Jews have also won significant sums of money from Germany and Switzerland, as well as other countries.

Can reparations "happen"?

On a repeat of the "Like It Is" program on ABC TV on August 12, 2001, the host, Gil Noble, once again dealt with the issue of reparations. He traced the history of the battle and spoke with Queen Mother Moore and Dudley Thompson, an attorney and former Jamaican ambassador.

Queen Mother Moore made the point that all aspects of the African's life has been affected by the establishment of slavery, including the way we look and the way we think.

Mr. Thompson discussed the fact that reparations is due to Africans throughout the world for the more than three hundred years of slavery. He emphasized that the first thing that the European needs to do is to apologize for the enslavement of the African and other peoples. He mentioned that reparations is not necessarily about giving money to Black people, but it's about forgiving debts to third world countries, as well as eliminating racist practices and leveling the playing field of opportunity for all people.

Other people spoke about the issue, including the representative of the December 12th Movement, who spoke of their advocacy of the issue to the United Nations.

This author believes that some form of reparations must take place before this issue will go away. The European has become rich and has had an easy life at the expense of the African and other peoples. There is a debt to pay. Notwithstanding the White man's protest that he is not responsible for the sins of his father, the fact is that the sin has been committed and confession and dissolution must take place in order for the sins to be forgiven.

Above all, it is imperative that we agitate, unceasingly, for reparations for the evil visited on our fore-parents in the form of chattel slavery, and on us, in the form of psychological and financial slavery. At the very least, our children should and must receive a free college education and the so-called "third world" debt be forgiven.

What We Must Do

Identify and Boycott Racist Businesses. Jews and other peoples make it a habit to not support organizations that they consider to be acting in opposition to themselves and their causes. It doesn't matter if this perception is true. They not only boycott such organizations, but they also publicize their disdain so that others of their clan, as well as the world, are aware of their actions. We must, likewise, identify and boycott people who, by their actions, marginalize and disrespect us.

There was an incident where this author heard a merchant call a person (in his own store) with whom he disagreed, a "nigger." I confronted him and he said, "I don't mean you. You are a Jamaican. You are not one of them!" To which I replied, "We are all Africans. So if you disrespect one of us, you disrespect all of us. So I will no longer buy anything here and I will make sure that no one whom I know patronizes you!" And I meant it. I did not enter that store after that day.

We cannot get respect unless we demand it, and we should never reward anyone for disdaining and disrespecting us.

Support Our Business and Professional People. Over the years, I've heard most doting parents tell their children "Go to school and study hard, so that you will be able to get a good, high-paying job." I've also heard those same parents say that they don't buy anything from Black businesses, and they do not go the Black doctors, lawyers, etc.

That being the case, how do they expect their well-educated offspring to find that well-paying job, unless they work for another ethnic group?

We have become our own worst enemies. We see the European as superior and we bow before his throne. We lose sight of the fact that it is we who have enriched the world with our hard work and ingenuity. But, because of our inferiority complex, we have become timid, self-hating persons.

It is not surprising that we hate ourselves, because we are bombarded with negative images of ourselves. But we must remember that those images are the ones projected by our oppressors, and we must reject them. We have to change our perceptions of ourselves and we have to teach our children their value.

So we have to support our business and professional people and encourage others to do likewise. How else are we going to overcome?

Buy 10%+ Within the Community. We have discussed, elsewhere, the value of spending at least ten percent of our disposable income within our community, but it bears repeating. We must spend at least that percentage of all the money we control within the community, in order to build it. We cannot expect others to do for us. We must do it for ourselves, and we can, if we follow the simple method of spending our resources.

The suggestion to spend ten percent is not written in stone. Some people will want to spend more. Some may want to start with less, and you won't be condemned for it. Some will be reluctant beginners, but will convert with a little urging. Still others will not do it, for a variety of reasons. Hopefully, we will get an average expenditure in excess of ten percent, as a beginning.

When this formula is put to work for us, one will be surprised at the financial level to which our community will be catapulted.

Hire Community People. When Black businesses are successful the recipient of the jobs are the people from the Black community. After all, it is our community that has the highest unemployment rate and so, has the highest available job applicants. It is also true that, even if our jobs were made available to everyone, a vast percentage of others would not apply for them, partly because they would not want to have a Black employer.

For those who seek employment from Black businesses, let me urge you not to take these employers for granted. There are people who go on job hunts in sneakers, with their pants falling off of them and who are otherwise unkempt, who expect Black businessmen to hire them because they are "brothers." To do that is to show a lack of respect.

Black businesspersons do, and must, expect the same level of presentation and professionalism that other employers do. They are in business to succeed and, if they don't, they will no longer exist and be an asset to the community. Black job hunters must dress for success, as do others. Very few people are going to consider hiring a person who is not appropriately attired because the lack of attention to one's attire most oftentimes represent the lack of attention to other things, including the job.

The job seeker must also be properly trained. Training should not only be in the specific area of need, but in the fundamentals of business theory and practice. It does help an employee to know how the business in which he/she is hired works. This information, at the very least, apprises them of how their input affects the company.

It is almost impossible, these days, for any business to operate without the utilization of a computer system. Therefore, it behooves any potential employee to learn and hone up on their computer skills at intervals. They make themselves more valuable to a business by doing so. The business entity may not have someone on staff to teach these skills, so the new employee with these skills may become "king (or queen) of the hill."

Weed Out "Bad" Professionals. It was previously mentioned that there is a lot of complaints in the Black community about the "professionals" and other workers. Most of these complaints are legitimate, except that they do not represent the actions of most entrepreneurs and workmen.

To the person who is "squeezed" or wronged, one bad egg is too many, so the problem cannot be ignored. And there are too many who prey on innocent people, both with respect of lack of value for their money and charging for work not done. Those people need to be eliminated. People need to take whatever actions are necessary against them and they should not be protected or coddled.

The business and professional people, as well as the victims, must all make a concerted effort to prevent these people from victimizing any new persons, in the future. They must take them to court, publicize their delinquency and thievery, and make sure that they are forced out of business. It pays to remember that in order for a person who has cancer to be cured, the cancer must be excised. Therefore, since that "bad" person represents a cancer, that person must be cut off in order for the good of the whole.

Help Ourselves. It is not easy for Black people to succeed in an economy that is skewed toward the rich, especially the White, people of the world. Therefore, we have to find ways to help ourselves get up and brush ourselves off. Some of the ways are mentioned elsewhere, but bear repeating:

Form Investment Groups. Pooling resources is an easier way to accumulate than patiently saving, and waiting, for the money to grow. If ten people pool resources, they can begin to invest in something far earlier than any one of them would be able to do. And the sooner that one begins to invest, the sooner one will begin to earn the reward of that investment and build wealth. So, investment groups are highly recommended for the not-so-well-off person who wants to build a nest-egg for retirement but does not get a large payment, or want to depend on, Social Security.

Investment groups also have another value in that people of like mind, coming together, have a geometric effect on the investment process. People benefit from brainstorming, and a good team can be "dynamite." It is also an instrument for socializing, and people who become "friends" thrive a little better than people operating in isolation.

The downside of the investment club model is that two or more people may want to dominate the group and may engender hard feelings amongst its members. The members must plan for this eventuality and expel disruptive members.

It is recommended that groups consider purchasing land. Land is the "gold-standard" for Black folk. It allows for a lot of flexibility and, when people are trying to "move" one, they must pay you for your land. If you rent you can be evicted without a fight. So buy land and, if the worst scenario occurs, you can always plant your tomato or your corn, etc.

Above all, you must shore up Black banks by depositing your money in them. Banks are where one goes to get a mortgage, a credit card, a car loan, a college loan, or money to bury a loved one, if all else fails.

One reason why the Black community is so poverty-stricken is that we put our money in banks that do not give us loans. Banks must protect their depositors' money and lend to "qualified" people. They do not give us loans, partly because they do not value our business, nor do they value our community. We are also "dissed" because we do not represent a large percentage of their depositors.

The more money the Black banks will have on deposit, the more flexible they will be in extending loans to people in our community. And the more money we will have for investment and other needs!

While you ponder, in our indecision about whether we can afford to spend the ten percent of our disposable income within our community, let me point out a final economic statistic to you. A 2010 study of wealth in the Black and White communities shows that at this time the average White family is worth $100,000.00 while the average Black family is worth only $5,000.00.

To reiterate, it's all about the money!

Section VI

Educational Participation

Who is to educate our children? In the book, *The Miseducation of the Negro*, Carter G. Woodson recognizes both the problem and the dilemma of the African American with regard to the European education system. He regards the system as totally flawed and suggests ways of circumventing it.

In the twenty-first century—one hundred and fifty years after "emancipation"—African Americans are still many steps behind their White "cousins" in the level of educational instruction and facility, as well as opportunity to make relevant adjustments to correct the problem.

Despite national initiatives—"charter school" drive, "no child left behind" and "race to the top"—Black children are losing ground. Children's under-education and mis-education continue. There are many reasons for this phenomenon.

Deliberate Mis-education in Order to Protect the Pie

There is the message, in certain quarters, that Black folks are inferior. This might be a vestige of

Darwin's *Theory of Evolution,* and the belief (I mean the hope) of some White folks that they are somewhat more evolved than Black folks, and so, they are, therefore, superior. The fact is that those who are intelligent enough know that this theory is flawed. If any one of the races is superior, it is the Black race. Consider our resilience through four centuries of slavery (physical and emotional), the fact that education was forbidden, and the result that we learned to read and write and invent and progress and rise....

Consider, also, that once given the chance, Blacks from Africa and the West Indies (even with less education) perform in a superior manner, and earn a higher standard of living than their White counterparts. One reason is that they are less brainwashed and, therefore, more self-confident. Another reason is the "immigrant mentality."

How, then, can the "masters" keep us in check? They must mis-educate us. They must convince us that they are more intelligent and, therefore, we are less intelligent. They must convince us that they are the inventors, the patriarchs of civilization, and they must steal our legacy (see *Stolen Legacy).* In order to induct and protect their indoctrination they must make sure that they control the educational tools, at all levels. They must make sure that they convince us, and we convince ourselves, that whatever they do is better, more valuable, more lasting. This is all done to protect the pie. If we find out that we are not inferior, we might want to get the better job, so that we can earn more, and be able to earn a bigger piece of the pie, thus leaving less for them and their offspring.

Even today, there are those, like the Texas Board (of Regents) who have voted to reduce the role of people like Thomas Jefferson who called for equality and the abandonment of slavery, and promote the "positive" influence of some racist "rebels." There are also people promoting the "New Orleans Model" of firing seasoned pedagogues and hiring, instead, inexperienced people from the business, and other fields, in order to "inject new blood into the system." That's double-speak for people who will stop teaching about ethnicity, etc.

We must change this system of mis-education, by letting the world know of our abilities and our accomplishments. It is not enough to know that something can be done. If one is to accomplish a goal, then one has to know the steps to take and how to take them, successfully.

In the book, *Think and Grow Rich: A Black Choice*, the authors emphasize the importance of goal-setting. They state:

> Every successful individual follows, in one form or another, the same goal-setting techniques. Some follow it diligently. Those who stand at the threshold of achievement have utilized goal-setting

> on a routine basis. You must do the same. Follow these instructions to the letter; comply with them in good faith, and remember that by doing so you are duplicating the procedure used by many of the greatest leaders this nation has ever produced. With pad and pencil, settle into a place where you feel comfortable—a favorite desk or chair—somewhere you feel creative. Plan to spend the next sixty minutes defining exactly what it is you expect to be, to do, or to create. It could very well be the most valuable sixty minutes of your life.

They go on to suggest that one write a clear, concise statement of what one wants in life; outline the plan for achieving this major goal; set a definite timetable for achieving the goal; and memorize the chief aim and goal and repeat them several times each day.

The Power Consideration

The greatest misconception in the minds of people of color is that racism is based on Black and White. The great motivator is the GREEN. The green is otherwise known as the ALMIGHTY DOLLAR. Do not misunderstand me! Racism is alive and well and living in America, and elsewhere. But the great petrol which fuels racism is "the green." If one doubts my assertion, one needs only to look at the building of America.

During the early years in the development of the "New World," the English elite was not willing to risk their lives and well-being in this unknown sector. But they wanted to have the place developed in order that they were provided with the taxes and the goods which were to be found in their new conquests. They decided to empty the prisons and the lunatic asylums and allow the inmates the opportunity for freedom if they would colonize the wilderness of North America. But they had to offer more than just the "freedom" to be imprisoned in this new land. They offered them freedom, as well as land, after a seven-year stint as an indentured servant.

The first Black "immigrants" to the New World were also brought as indentured servants. (Let me remind the reader that, according to Ivan van Sertima's book, *They Came Before Columbus*, and other sources, evidence of African visitors to the Americas dates back many hundreds of years before the visit of Christopher Columbus.)

However, because Blacks were considered more suitable for hard work and because they could not "melt" into the population, the powers-that-be decided that they should not be released after the seven years, but rather be made into permanent chattel slaves. The decision-makers rightfully believed that there would be no outcry from anyone if they just declared the "colored" man to be inferior, thus justifying his treatment as less than human and his ultimate enslavement. So the decision to enslave was an economic one.

There was, in fact, precedence for this economic decision. Prior to the enslavement of Blacks in the United States, the "great humanitarian" priest Bartholomew de las Casas had recommended to the Spanish throne that the captive "Indians" were not productive. They were killing themselves rather than remain in bondage, so Negroes should be imported from Africa to do the hard labor and enrich Spain and Portugal.

So, it is about money *and power*, which go hand-in-hand. *The golden rule is really that he who hath the gold, rules.* The old adage states that he who controls your paycheck controls you. It is not surprising, then, that the White population wishes to, and insists on, controlling the education of the so-called minority population.

Although the media is the most obvious means of control of power, the educational system is the most profound. Black and White children have different educational focuses. White children learn of how the Europeans transformed the world from darkness and depravity to one where everyone is able to live a luxurious, enlightened life. They are told that while the other peoples were uncivilized, they were inventing the steam engines, electricity, the mathematical systems, exploring space and time with their Greek philosophy, Roman law and architecture, English organization and genius, and Catholicism, just to mention a few things.

Black children are taught that the caucasian has done all of these things which, if they were lucky, a few of them would be able to enjoy, with their good jobs and their spending power. And they would be able to leave the ghetto and spend time in the white hotels and stores, etc. To this day, Whites are trained to be the bosses and Blacks are trained to be good servants and consumers.

What is not told is that Blacks have a lackadaisical attitude to hoarding because they lived in areas of the world that were rich in both vegetation and ore and they learned to share because there was always more than enough to go around. They mostly lived communal lives in which everyone shared in the protection and interest of everyone else.

Europeans, on the other hand, lived in areas of sparsity, where there were short growing seasons and dire climactic conditions, and so they developed a need to protect the limited resources and guard the food from their neighbors. This is the way that they acquired their need for acquisition and their yen for warmongering. There was a declaration of war of all against all.

These traits were honed and expanded to the point that most Europeans seem to feel that everything belongs to them and that no other peoples have a right to anything in the world that they have a desire for. That is why they can come to the United States from European countries not having themselves, or their forefathers, contributed one iota to the building of America, and demand every benefit for themselves, to the exclusion of African Americans (and Native Americans), who have built this country with their sweat and blood.

Lack of Commitment—Teachers' Children in Private Schools

Another important contributor to the decline in education, especially in the African American community is the lack of commitment on the part of our teachers.

Let me begin by saying that this is not an indictment of good, dedicated teachers. And there are many. However, this is meant to deal with a serious problem.

There was a time when people chose professsions to which they were drawn, and took pride in the excellent performance of those jobs. Today, the vast majority of people are only concerned about whether the job is available and how much compensation they can reap from the position. The teaching profession is no exception.

The disgrace, which many teachers seem to perpetrate on the public school system, is that too many send their children to private schools, while collecting a salary from the public school system. How much more of a lack of confidence can one display than to pay for one's children to attend school in the private sector while not only paying taxes for a public sector education but being also a part of that system? Such an action displays a lack of confidence, not only in one's colleagues, but also in oneself.

Such decision to privately educate one's children also displays a lack of commitment to improve the system. If the educator in question had that commitment s/he would fight to improve educational standards in order to not only provide the offspring with a first-class education, but also to add to his/her job security by making sure that the system does not fail.

But the problem is deeper than the foregoing insinuations may suggest! The fact is that the public school educators, with their charges who are, for the most part so-called minority students, are either of the belief that the students are inferior, or they know that the students can learn but are part of the conspiracy to under-educate or mis-educate these youngsters.

If they are contributors to the theory of inferiority, they may think that any extra effort would be a waste of their time. And if they are just racist, they may have made the conscious decision not to educate them properly and, thereby, put a lie to their assertions that these students are inferior.

In either case, a great many teachers do not want to educate these so-called minority students and allow them to be in a position to compete with their own children for the limited resources.

These types of teachers are a disgrace to their profession and are a blight on their country because they are not allowing the proper development of the human resources that are needed to propel the constant growth and development of the country.

The result is that some of the potentially best brains in the United States are not allowed to develop and America is losing intellectual ground to the rest of the world.

The Profit Margin—Textbooks, Supplies, Consultants

Another reason why the education system stagnates, is that some of the financial resources are pilfered.

Consider, for example, the cost of textbooks to an educational institution. Whereas the cost to produce a textbook may be $2.00 and would be sold as a trade book for $10.00 to $12.95, once it is adopted as a textbook, its price may jump to $35.00

or $50.00. The reason: the publisher now has a captive market, and is no longer concerned about selling the book at a competitive price. Furthermore, whereas a bookstore may be sold that book, in the first instance, at a 35%-40% discount, the textbook discount is 0% to 20%. The publisher no longer has to give the bookseller an incentive to sell the particular book because all s/he has to do is "make it and they will buy." After all, the administrators are not spending their own money, they reason, and they **must** buy textbooks. The same scenario can be repeated with respect to school supplies and consultants. The result of this gouging is that less training aids end up in the classrooms, where they belong.

The greedy producers, meanwhile, increase their normal profit margins from the 300-400 percent to maybe 1000 percent.

Privatization

In a further, concerted effort to destroy public education, the conservatives (and racists) are pushing for privatization, under the ploy that the system will be operated more efficiently. And President Obama is falling for it! But like all private entities, the operations are streamlined to benefit the private investor, not the interest of the client. The idea of public education is to provide training for the general populace, not the enrichment of a few greedy individuals. Two forms that privatization takes are the Voucher program and Charter Schools.

A government is the entity that is supposed to operate in the public interest and act as a conduit to guarantee the involvement and benefit of all individuals, no matter from what "class" or ethnic group they emanate. It is, therefore, necessary for the government to be involved in certain areas in order to guarantee said involvement and protection of those souls who are either less able or unable to take care of themselves. That responsibility is not the purview of private enterprise. Under those circumstances, and given the models of private schools, with their need to operate at a profit, it is foolhardy and defeating of the purpose of public education, for the school system to be "privatized."

The new push for privatization, beginning in about 2001, came directly from the Bush White House. In Republican style, the administration pushed the so-called voucher program, ostensibly to help poor and middle-class Americans to allow their children to go to preparatory schools and be able to compete with the rich. Supposedly, this method of funding will bring equity to the system. But let us ask the million-dollar question. Who will really benefit from the transfer of funds from public to private educational institutions? The answer is simple—the rich!

First of all, the amount of each voucher does not pay tuition to the average private school. So most poor children will not get in. Furthermore, the schools will select the students, not the parents select the school. This method of, as they believe, funding education will allow for credit to the rich for the money they spend in private schools, including the additional credits they will get for their voucher entitlements.

The next outcome is that the funds are drained from public schools and they will become defunct. For those doubters I present to you the present dilemma. There is the push to close "non-functioning" public schools. What about non-functioning private schools? No! They change the principals, change the teachers, and change the students, if necessary. But not the schools! Now they close the public schools! What they are doing is privatize these schools and fund their owners with the money that should have been funneled to the public schools. Arne Duncan and Barack Obama need to be concerned about this!

Who really determines which are non-functioning schools and how can that be "properly" determined when the push is on test-taking and not on instruction?

Do we expect to see the students returned to these institutions? They will not. The new management chooses the students who will help to guarantee them triumph and prove the voucher program a success.

Under the banner of "No Child Left Behind," and the "Son" Bush administration, hell has broken loose on public education. A number of things have happened:

Using their "faith-based initiative", billions of public dollars have been transferred to religious organizations. Why? What about the Constitutional separation of church and state? The authors of the Constitution were very astute and thoughtful in writing the document. I'm sure that they considered the history of religious persecution by the governments and "Church" in Europe and wanted to avoid such entanglements in the United States. They, probably, also considered that the U.S. is a country that had welcomed people of all religious faiths, so there could be a grave problem with the domination of one religion over others.

We will note that while most of the signers of the Constitution presented themselves as religious, prayers were not included in the schools and other public places. The phrase, "In God We Trust" is seen everywhere. But the belief must have been that, whatever one's religion, we "all" trust in God.

In 2007, we found the rise of the "Charter" schools in full swing throughout the country, but especially in New York City. The Charter School bedazzles parents (who want the best for their children) to reach for a better option to the failing public school system, so that their children can obtain maximum educational benefit. And the Charter Schools are showing improved performance because of those children who are accepted. The problem, though, is that only the brightest children are accepted.

The second result is that there is a "brain drain" on the public school from which these students are taken and so, it is not surprising when the "overall" performance of that school drops.

The third consideration is that, within the first (three?) years of their operation, these Charter Schools are not required to accept children in need of "remediation" or ones with special needs, so the level of their success is suspect. How will they sustain their boastful successes when they become responsible for lesser qualified students? Time will tell, but the public school system does not have that time. It will be destroyed by the time the farce of the Charter School becomes obvious.

According to reliable sources, the New York City Department of Education (on the instructions of the Mayor, one suspects) allotted nearly forty percent of its 2008 budget for Charter Schools (including the building and renovation fund). When one considers that so many public schools are being closed (especially in the so-called Minority areas) and the buildings are being turned over to private individuals (sometimes for $1.00 per year rental), one should be appalled and alarmed. And it is *the children* who are being evicted from their neighborhood schools!

The public school system in America, as we know it, will be totally ruined.

Now why should we be so concerned about the system? Well, children of color, as well as poor children in general, will be left uneducated, with the result that our community will be lost. The private system will concentrate on educating the "majority" population. There will be no more bilingual bridge programs, no more remedial programs, and no enhancement programs for those students who have special needs, because the money won't be available.

Just as happened with the HMO's, teachers might be paid incentives to not refer students for remediation, because that will cost the system too much money. Racism will dictate what happens in the system.

The Ebonics Controversy— Modern-Day Smokescreen

Much ado has been made in recent years about the use of "ebonics" in the Black community. Ebonics is classified as the method of speech that is used instead of "standard" English. The theorists, as would be expected, differ in terms of their perceptions concerning the benefits and drawbacks of the use of such a dialect in the school system.

On the one hand, the proponents feel that the curriculum should be modified to allow for instruction in the "language" to which the students are familiar. Thus, they argue, the students will have a better understanding of what is being told to them and will, consequently, be better prepared for the many tests which they are given. It is argued that they cannot progress if they do not understand what they are being told in "the Queen's English."

These people argue that no attention should be paid to standard grammar but, instead, to the content of the students' work which shows an understanding of what they should be learning.

The second school of thought is that ebonics is totally ruinous to the student and should be abandoned, at school and at home, in favor of standard grammar and that grading should be weighted in favor of the latter.

They argue that it is almost impossible that a person, once corrupted by ebonics, will make the transference to instruction in standard English and, therefore, instruction would be wasted.

While it is true that the use of ebonics does, sometimes, stifle learning in a standard setting, the "language" is a major communications tool for the practitioners, and should not be abandoned. People of color, and particularly Black people, have always needed a language of communication that is unfamiliar to the oppressor, in order to survive. It has to be an ever-changing language, because the oppressor is always learning the codes so as to understand and keep the oppressed in their places.

It is also important that all Black people become fluent in the language of the oppressor because, only by doing so can we decipher the codes of oppression and keep ahead of the evil which it accompanies. One of the great White "liberators" is alleged to have said that if White people wanted to hide some knowledge, they need only put it in a book. The ridiculous truth of this statement is that, at the time of the remark, it was illegal for Black people to learn to read. So it was illegal for them to explore the sources of information!

Knowing the language also allows us to learn the things that will give us the foundation upon which to build the structure for our emancipation.

The ebonics "discussion" detracts from the fact that the schools in the Black community are underfinanced, over-crowded, equipment-poor, and sometimes lack competent pedagogues. It is a wellspring of enrichment for people who are known as the "welfare pimps," especially those who benefit from steering Black children into special education classes, thereby guaranteeing extra positions for themselves and their colleagues. In this way they can be nonproductive and blame their futility on the intellect of the children who cannot understand because they are steeped in ebonics. Some of the most educated Black people are versed in ebonics.

The Failure of Students

In a large percentage of instances, students fail to get a proper education because of their own lack of ambition, peer pressure and failure to persist when faced with obstacles. They are, sometimes, also unmotivated because of their environments.

While it is understandable that Black students will be "turned off" by the prospect of a wasted future and the futility of spending many years of studiousness when the result will be working for someone who makes half their contributions at twice the pay, it is, nevertheless, critically important that they exercise the discipline to absorb the information.

Students also feel that they must like the teacher in order to learn, or they feel that all teachers know what they are "talking about" so the information is gospel, and is to be accepted, unquestioningly. That is not so.

School is supposed to prepare the students to not only spew out the information that is taught, but to emerge as thinking, reasoning beings. We all know many educated fools—those who flaunt the fact that they have Ph.D. degrees, but have not the reasoning capability of a six-year-old child.

It is urged that students understand the importance of their education and to not let anyone stifle their opportunities for excellence. They must hold their teachers to excellence in their preparation and instruction, and they must hold their peers to strict behavior in the classroom. They must be made to understand that one of the major causes of mediocrity in the education system is that instruction is wasted, due to students' disruption in the classroom.

Those disruptive students cheat their peers of the information that they need and cause them to get a lesser understanding of the subject at hand and, thus, lower grades.

In short, students need to be more proactive in their education.

Building Self-Esteem and Empowering Students

The most important ingredient to success is a high self-esteem. Unfortunately, that is the one ingredient which most Black people—and, indeed, most Black children—lack in their quest for excellence. The cause of this dearth is many-fold.

From the day of birth Black children are bombarded with images of White people performing great acts of importance to society. These people are portrayed as the doctors and the nurses who "deliver" us at birth; as the day-care center directors and teachers; as the religious school teachers and ministers; as the teachers and principals at school; as the local political leaders, mayors, governors and presidents; as the local bankers and business persons; as the policemen, lawyers and judges; and as the captains of entertainment, among other things. In short, we are introduced to them as the leaders of the world.

Black people, on the other hand, are portrayed as the criminals; as the high-school dropouts; as the welfare recipients; as the beggars; as the retards of the world. We are not given credit as the inventors of almost everything that is beneficial to the present-day human beings (although improvements to some of the inventions may have been done by others).

They are not given credit for inventions which others have stolen, including the light bulb (the invention for which Thomas Edison got credit) and the cotton gin, for which Eli Whitney received the accolades, just to name a couple.

Black children must be made aware of the role of their ancestors and their other fellow Blacks who must be held up as role models to them. They must be made to understand that they are also capable, by reason of their intellect, of accomplishing whatever they set their minds to, in spite of whatever obstacles are placed in their paths.

Only by becoming aware of their own potential, as well as the contributions of others of their race, will Black students—and Black people—make the kind of progress of which we are capable.

The Failure of Parents

Parents fail their children in many ways.

Unfortunately, parenting does not come with an operating manual and so most parents do not know how to handle the job. Therefore, the quality of parenting runs the gamut from excellent to "piss poor." Most parents delegate their jobs to their own parents, the government, the teachers, the gangs, the military, and the police. Then they complain that they have done their best, but their children have either disappointed or disgraced them.

The first mistake which parents make is to believe and act as if the children are their pals who they want to love them. Therefore, they will not chastise these children because it will be traumatic for the children. The catch-words are "child abuse." Whereas I will not say that there are not many abusive parents, I advocate a good spanking when it is well deserved. My parents used it, as did theirs—for generations—and we may have hurt for a short while, but it has been valuable to our generations. Dr. Spock be damned! He and his theory have messed up the world. Now children have no respect for man or God, and are parenting the parents.

Furthermore, with the criminal "justice" system "criminalizing" our children, we need to emphasize discipline at home rather than allow the system to slaughter them, literally and figuratively. We cannot be dissuaded by a stunning court ruling in Atlanta, which allowed well-disciplined children to be taken away from loving, caring parents and put into homes where there were proven cases of abuse. In that case, the parents and the minister administered corporal punishment to children they thought were deserving of such "severe" punishment. They were charged with child abuse. Even though an investigation showed that these families were much more stable than others and that the children were well-adjusted youngsters, some of the children were never returned, because the parents refused to compromise in their successful methods of child-rearing. So they were punished, and the children are victims of the government. Those parents are not failing their children, but the system is!

The second mistake is the giving of our children to the school system for indoctrination. We need our children educated, but we must be involved in their education. We must become involved with the PTAs and the school staff, and communicate to them our expectations for our children and the role they are to play in making sure that those goals are reached. We must also inform them of the penalties for their failure to meet these goals—removal from their positions.

We must become sufficiently politically powerful to carry out these promises. We must also, most importantly, make sure that most of our children's instructors are like them because, next to parents, teachers serve most as role models.

The third error which parents commit is allowing the media to rear their children. The media is the tool of the oppressor and, as mentioned previously, it distorts the news to the detriment of people of color. It preaches the supremacy of the White race and the inferiority—to a lesser or greater extent—of all other races. How can we expect our children to have a high self-esteem when they are so mis-educated from the beginning. How can be expect them to have a yen for knowledge and the perseverance to pursue excellence, when we allow such destruction of their intellect? We are their keepers and we must prevent these occurrences.

The fourth mistake which parents make is to allow the "government" to usurp their authority as parents. The government has become involved in the daily life of children. To avoid discipline the child needs only to call the child welfare division in any municipality and parents can be arrested for the slightest presumed infraction of child-rearing. Yet the selfsame "government" does not hesitate to incarcerate these children for presumed infractions on their part, having "tried" them as adults.

Empowering Staff—and Parents

There was a time when parents were considered to be an asset to the school system. That time has passed. Today, parents are considered by the system to be nuisances who don't know anything about education and are themselves mostly uneducated—but want to tell these educated teachers and administrators how to do their jobs.

The time when parents were valued by the educational system was the time when teachers were proud of their profession and wished to do an extraordinary job of educating children. Today, for too many educators, it is only about the paycheck. Furthermore, many administrators, especially at the highest levels, do not have education on their minds. So parent involvement would be a liability for them! Their interest is in maximizing their exposure so that they can get a "cushy" job when they retire, or in just maintaining the *status quo.*

There are educators who don't want parents around to see their ineptitude, and see their colleagues who are performing at a higher level and make comparisons. Parent involvement promotes teacher commitment, and many teachers are not ready to commit to excellence in education.

Likewise, staff empowerment becomes a problem to both staff and administrators. Some staff members don't want the responsibility or the extra work of their empowerment. Why should they spend extra time, or expend extra effort, when they could be concentrating on their own affairs?

Administrators, also, discourage staff empowerment for various reasons. Sometimes, it is because they see themselves as management, with the staff being obedient laborers who should never question their authority. Sometimes, though, they may be afraid of the staff input because it may reveal or accentuate their lack of competence, or lessen their authority.

Whatever the problems, challenges, or other reasons, it is imperative to the educational system that parents, staff and administrators all work together in order to provide the best education for their charges.

Many years ago, in New York City (especially around Oceanhill-Brownsville, in Brooklyn), there was a number of protest marches, as well as other actions, which culminated in the decentralization of the New York City Board of Education. The result was the forming of the basic 32-district Board which, under that structure, called for the election of nine-member School Boards, which would have significant input into the educational system and, therefore, over the education of their children.

Needless to say, this system was overturned, due to the persistence of some centralists who wanted to regain control, and the ineptness and “alleged” corruption of many School Board members. Of note is the fact that, even in areas where the dominant population was African American, these Boards were mostly controlled by Europeans, because the Black population failed to vote in School Board elections, as they fail to do in other elections. So the system has reverted to the control of the people who see the education system only for the fact that there is an approximately $21 billion budget which should not be controlled by anyone but them.

Likewise, our failure to get involved in the schools, via the PTAs, leave our children ignorant and vulnerable. There are instances where the student body of a school may be one thousand, yet the attendance at the PTA meeting is less than ten. It is no wonder that the powers that be do not take us seriously and, consequently, they do not nourish and educate our children.

So what can we do? We must insist that since we are the guardians of our children we must have significant involvement in their lives and their education. We must be heard!

We must also advocate for more input by the classroom teacher and other staff. An edict should not be sent down from headquarters, to be followed, unquestioningly, by the peons at the school level. The "foot soldiers" are more aware of many important on-the-spot challenges and opportunities than any of the generals could ever imagine. So they need to be heard, and some of their ideas should be incorporated into the planning.

The Failure of Government

The government (at all levels) has almost always failed people of color—except Asians—in terms of preparation for and enforcement of the educational process.

The history of the United States is one in which it was, in fact, illegal for Blacks to be taught or to learn to read. Even after the end of slavery when the manumitted population was allowed to make their own decisions about their future, the country did not, nor did the states, provide for the education of these people. But they did provide for the education of the majority population.

Later, when the government did elect to allow for public education of African Americans, they made no effort to provide for equal educational opportunities and, indeed, there was evidence of overt opposition to equally educating this segment of the population.

Finally, with the settlement of the lawsuit of Brown vs. Board of Education in the 1954 landmark decision, African Americans were supposed to be offered equal educational opportunities in shared environments. However, because of the fact of segregation at all levels of racial interaction, there was no way that this law could be enforced.

This rift was not even narrowed by the 1964 civil rights bill which was signed into law by President Johnson, nor by any other legislation which should have allowed for people of all races to have access to all aspects of opportunities available in the United States.

A final restriction is that the American society is still segregated along racial lines. Communities are still separated along racial lines and so, school districts are drawn along those same racial lines.

One of the ways the government attempted to handle the discrepancy in educational opportunities between the races was the system of busing. This remedy was in vogue in the 1960s and early 1970s, but has fallen out of favor in recent years for obvious reasons. Busing presented many problems that are not easily resolved.

It is very difficult on the children who are bused. First of all, they spend many more hours per week in travel to and from school and have much less time for rest and for extra-curricular activities. Secondly, they are put in a new environment, away from their families and friends, and with people whom they don't know. The third problem is that they are usually not welcome in the new environment by the people who do not know anything about them nor want to know anything about them. Finally, even where there is an attempt to teach these "immigrant" students, the new teachers do not understand them and their learning styles and therefore, are usually unsuccessful in their venture.

But let's not digress from the factors involved. Even where laws are enacted to provide educational opportunities for Blacks, the enforcement is not provided and, therefore, there is no chance for the benefits to be accrued. This lack of enforcement effort is pervasive at all levels of government in the United States. We see a great deal of wasted brainpower in this country, especially when we take a good look at the dynamic contributions of Black people—in spite of the limited access to education which we have had over the centuries.

Textbooks and Supplementary Materials

Although there is a great increase in the number and types of material available to public school children, there is still a dearth of material to build self-esteem and encourage excellence in the classroom and in life. We still have *Dick and Jane* type stories with which African American and other inner-city children cannot relate.

And I don't mean the types of books that have no place in the classroom, with subject matters that only parents should have a right to discuss with young children, **whenever they choose.** I mean relevant, historical truths, rather than the erroneous information given in most history books.

Textbooks and supplementary materials, which are used in the educational system, must begin to reveal the truth about the experiences of all people, instead of the embellished history of one people and the misinformation about the other peoples.

Thinking about the "historical facts" in most of these textbooks remind me of the story of the lion and the mouse. A gentleman was telling his little son the story of how the lion and the mouse had a battle and how the mouse "whipped" the lion, to which the little boy asked, "Dad, the lion is a big, strong animal, and the mouse is small and weak. How could the mouse beat the lion?" The father replied that the story was told, by the mouse, and that when it is told by the lion, the outcome will be completely different. If anyone has any doubts about "historical facts" one has only to look at occurrences in the world, and how some nations, even when they are the aggressors, are portrayed as the victims. Some of the people who are terrorized are called terrorists.

Christopher Columbus "discovered" the habitat of the Native Americans and later the Europeans slaughtered the "savages" and "brought civilization to the Americas". So the story goes! But how about the true story that these Natives were civilized because they acted in a civil manner when they invited the strangers in, kept them from dying in the harsh winters, taught them to plant and fish, only to be massacred and have their land stolen. Whose story is true and more credible? It depends of who writes it and who learns and believes it.

The truth must be told that the "Great White Father" with the forked tongue murdered the Native Americans, in cold blood, and stole their land, so there should be reparations to them. People of conscience must insist on it. The Native Americans were not savages. They had highly developed cultures. Their problem was that they did not have highly developed weapons. The facts must come out that America is great because of the significant and varied contributions of its mosaic of people.

The truth must be told about how the Europeans gathered together to divide Africa amongst themselves and enslave its people and how, after they "returned their freedom", they still have these Africans economically and legally enslaved because they still control their economics and their legal systems. Look at the case of South Africa that, under apartheid, had nuclear power but, as part of its "liberation", had to sign it away. Its economics and its land are still controlled by the same racist rats.

Even if we cannot tell the truth in such stark, harsh language, we must tell it, rather than continue to perpetrate and perpetuate the lie.

That is why it is so important that Black people have a say in the education of our children. So that we can also tell them our story!

So, how can we be of benefit to the educational system that so powerfully impacts our children and, therefore, our future? We need to recruit the help of all of our resources.

Educate Our Own Children

There are many thousands of African American parents who are opting to educate their own children, either in an African-centered educational setting, or through home-schooling.

More and more, this seems like the only way that we are going to guarantee that our children are not emotionally damaged and their self-esteem corrupted. No one can do the job of educating one's children as that parent can, as long as that parent has done the required preparation.

A knowledgeable parent can intermix facts with circumstances, so that a child can have a better understanding of what the conditions were which influenced a decision, or the influences one had in coming to that decision. A knowledgeable parent can help a child to develop thinking skills that, after all, should be the ultimate goal of education.

A wise parent will, however, not neglect the history of the dominant culture, especially as it impacts the state of the student and his/her family.

Twelve Ways to Help a Child Learn to Read

The following are some of the recommended ways to help a child master reading and thinking skills:

1. Start reading to the child at a very early age. He/she may not be able to understand, at first, but he/she will get used to seeing you with books, and it will become natural for the child to read.

2. Have the child "read" to you, even before he/she knows how. Use bright picture books, so that the story can be memorized and the child read the pictures. This early confidence will help the child to read sooner. One must, therefore, correct the children when they err, and praise them for every effort.

3. Associate the printed page with familiar objects. For example, if one reads about apples or oranges, show the child the representation of the written word. In addition, identify things in the community as you walk with the child. Identify the red, yellow and green of the traffic light; the stop

sign to reinforce s-t-o-p; etc. This makes stories more real to the child.

4. Read books that reflect the children's "image" so that they can "claim" the knowledge. Most "minority" children cannot identify with Dick and Jane.

5. Take children to bookstores and libraries and have them help to choose books.

6. Learn the children's area(s) of interest and get books, slightly above their reading levels, which deal with those topics. Other books should be at or slightly below their level.

7. Discuss the material or story you have read to the child or which the child has read to you. Have the child repeat the story in his or her own words, and ask what it means.

8. Help children to rewrite stories, as well as writing their own. This will help develop their understanding, and thinking skills.

9. Instill the rewards of reading into the child. Use examples, such as the fact that it opens up "worlds" which the child would not otherwise experience.

10. Use role models, where possible. Expose the child to authors, and to other people who are successful in their fields of endeavor. These people become real, and inspirational and, further, this encourages reading.

11. Let the child know that some things will be more difficult than others, and that everyone has difficulty in one area or another. Therefore, when something becomes difficult, he/she needs to work harder, and seek help, instead of giving up.

12. Above all, one must be involved in the child's school, as well as other activities. When the child knows that parents and teachers are in contact, more attention is paid, not only to conduct, but to learning, as well. Besides, children always try harder if they know that the significant adults in their lives truly care about their welfare.

I'm sure others can come up with at least another twelve things, so the more, the better.

Be a Volunteer Tutor

There are thousands of retired teachers in our community, as well as those who are currently involved in the education system, who can add significant benefit to the youngsters who are in need of help and remediation. In addition, there are many thousands of people in various and varied professions who can instruct youngsters in their areas of expertise, if only they will volunteer the time to help.

All one needs to do is to allot a period of time per week or per month to help people who are in need of education, instruction or advice. It requires dedicating one hour or five hours or ten hours per month to helping to impart knowledge and skill to people who can then help to build the community and the nation.

Imagine how valuable your contribution would be if you help one youngster to get a job, or help one person to understand a math problem and so pass an exam, which he/she would otherwise have failed? Both you and the recipient will have benefited. And it doesn't take much of your time!

Advocate for Public Education

As taxpayers, we all pay for public education. Don't we? How many of us do not mind paying for the same thing more than once? That is what we are doing when we pay taxes to support the public education system, and then send our children to private schools. It is true that some people can afford to do that because they have the financial wherewithal. However, there are some Black folks who struggle with two jobs and sacrifice some of the necessities of life, in order to ensure that their children get a first-class private education.

As a parent, the author made every effort to make sure that his children were all "properly" educated, so it doesn't seem strange that some parents will not take chances with their children's education. However, as an advocate for public education I had to be sure to work toward strengthening the system and make sure that my children were afforded the maximum benefit available.

One of the major problems with the public school system is the non-involvement of parents. They don't attend PTA meetings; they don't come to open-school meetings with the teachers; they don't come to performances in which their children are involved; they don't get involved in fund-raising. However, part of the requirements for children's acceptance into private schools, is that the parents must be involved. So there is no recourse but to conclude that part of the success of private school is parent involvement, while part of the failure of public school is lack of involvement. Therefore, if parents were to put the same level of effort into making their children successful in public schools, as they are willing to put into the private schools, then the public schools would be an astounding success story.

So, parents, get off your collective asses and make your children's public schools work for them!

Weed Out "Bad", Non-caring Educators

As in any profession, most people involved in the school system are there for the paycheck (and the vacation time). They have no interest in education or in the children who they are hired to educate. There are even some who disdain the children and can't wait to get away from those disgusting, despicable kids.

Education, above all professions, demands love, patience, and dedication. Young minds are being molded, so one has to consider what they are doing to be an important task in order to do a good job at it. They need to have the patience to re-invent the wheel, so to speak, in finding the method that works for each child, since we all have different learning styleş and so, it is not one method fits all.

There are people who just have bad attitudes about life, relationships, etc. We do not want them influencing children. The damage can be irreparable. We do not want those who molest children or teach them depravity, because our children will be lost to us. So we must eliminate those people.

There are people entering the teaching profession because they have failed in the business and professional worlds. The education system is the last bastion of hope for their wretched souls. Pedagogy is an alien, dirty word to them. Yet they have our precious jewels in their claws. We must identify them and free them from their miserable existence in the classroom before they destroy themselves and the school.

If parents do not protect their children, no one will, so parents must be forever vigilant in protecting the intellect and the person of their children by making sure that the purity of the classroom setting is not polluted by these miscreants of educational aspirations.

Demand Government Funding at Appropriate Levels

In the State of New York, for example, there is a severe discrepancy in the funding for education within New York City and the rest of the state. The formula used to fund education is skewed toward the parts of the state that, not insignificantly, have a lesser proportion of people of color.

The governor and the state legislature are responsible for ascertaining that equity is granted and maintained and, if they don't do their jobs, heads should roll. Of course, in this case, the upstate voters participate in the voting process and so they get the lion's share of the pie. The downstate voters boycott the process and so they get the crumbs.

It is up to the taxpayers and voters of the state, as well as all the other states, to make sure that the politicians divvy up the taxes in the proper manner, to the benefit of all the constituents.

It is because Blacks don't get involved and make demands why we don't get our due. Education costs money and we pay taxes, so we should get the taxes working for us in the form of a proper education to our children. Nothing less will do!

Involve Businesses and Community Organizations in Education

Presently (in the year 2010), many corporations are interested in the education of children in America and they contribute in varied ways and in different amounts. Most are involved because they realize that the educational standard of the work pool is dwindling while the requirements are increasing. This has become a more advanced, technological world, where one has to meet more stringent demands for computer and related skills, and where other countries are outstripping America in their preparedness.

More and more, America has had to import talent from abroad, whether it be scientists, doctors, nurses, teachers, engineers, or other technocrats. So people have begun to sit up and take note. For the most part, however, this attention to educational level has just barely trickled down to the Black community. In the first place, we do not have the large businesses, with the deep pockets, to contribute to our educational development and, secondly, we have not considered the problem to be as serious as it is and so we have not begun to seek the proper solutions.

The problem is very serious and we must act with due diligence. We do not need to invest money in the educational system, so much as we need to invest time and energy and influence. We need to let the powers that be know that they will have a fight on their hands if they don't invest time, effort and money in our children.

Having said that, it must be added that it does warm my heart that there is such an increased involvement of businesses in the educational system. Where that involvement is "pure" it can go a long way to lifting the system out of the doldrums, especially when they are involved with "inner-city" schools.

Companies like Microsoft are contributing training and equipment to students, some of whom might not have had the opportunity to be exposed to the high-tech world of computers and the like. Other companies are exposing them to business and finance, while still others are introducing them to law and other fields of endeavor.

The experience with the business world can be invaluable to students, especially if part of the package includes some experience in the work-a-day world of the business "empire".

It will orient students on what really happens in the real life of a worker and will help to prepare them for the many challenges to be faced in the adult world. After all, school is just one place that prepares a child for success as an adult.

Businesses benefit from the contact with potential workers in many ways. Students get introduced to business before they become adults, stressed by the need to earn a living, sometimes in a loathing environment. In other words, it is generally a win/win situation. The only down side is that some businesses use this forum to advance their own ideologies and unduly profit from the interchange, while damaging the public education system.

We have proven that we are able to learn and perform. One has only to look at the Black youth who are involved in the drug or prostitution trade to see how well they can organize and conduct business, how intelligent and astute they are, and how successful they can be at an endeavor. Given the opportunity to learn and to conduct legitimate enterprises, they will also excel.

Involve the "Family" in Education

Teaching is family business! The education of each family member is the business of every other family member. There are many things that should be taught by the family members—including the extended family—but there are other things which children need to learn in a formal educational setting, along with their peers. This is where the school comes into play.

However, family, remember that just because the child is in school, there is no need for you to sit back and relax and leave it to the school (and the teachers) because some of the worst garbage is taught in school. The schools should not be party to lies like Santa Claus, the Easter Bunny, and the Halloween crap, for example. And we have already discussed the lies about history, which are told in school. We know that teachers of conscience have been terminated for teaching children the truth about Black history. So, we must learn it and teach it to our children and grandchildren, and brothers and sisters, and nieces and nephews, etc.

We must continue the oral traditions and we must strengthen family bonds, so that the children will listen to us. And we must let the educators know that we are strong and united families and we will do what it takes to ascertain that our children be given the quality education they deserve to have. The powers that be will be forced to take notice and act in the right way.

Contribute Financially to Education

It has been suggested, elsewhere, that all of us have an obligation to contribute to the education of all the others, especially the children. It is recognized that we can contribute our time and knowledge to this venture and that we all have talents that can be beneficial to ourselves, and to others, even though we don't always recognize these talents. In addition to talents, some of us have a little cash which we can "spare" for such a worthy cause.

Most things cost money! And money is the commodity that seems the most lacking in the Black community. However, we must spare a few of our dollars to financially support our educational institutions. As the UNCF motto goes, "A mind is a terrible thing to waste." Especially when we have given, and have so much more to offer, to the world!

So we must "stretch our purse strings" and support our Black educational organizations in order to continue to produce the diamonds, which we have been doing, in spite of the oppression we have encountered in education, as in all other areas. The sacrifice of our precious dollars will be worth the rewards of the better preparation for the world, which our offspring will have.

Teach Cooperative Economics

As the reader might have noticed, it is not my argument that all education will be administered by the school system. Nor can that ever be the case! Education starts at home and, quite frankly, the family is failing children in many ways. Most of us do not prepare our children to be successful.

If most of the preparation is about their being able to earn and to take good care of themselves and their family, how come we don't teach them about the most important thing to our future—"cooperative economics?"

Although the premise of economics are clearly delineated in the "Economics" section, it is worth noting here that Black children need to learn, early in their lives, the concept of money—how to earn it, how to retain it, and how to invest it. We are rapidly losing economic ground. Considering that we started at the bottom, we're in really bad shape.

We must discuss the family budget with our children, as soon as they are able to fully understand (they don't need to know every detail of everything), and explain the need to budget and to save. We must give them allowances and help them to budget. We must encourage them to become conscious consumers and serious entrepreneurs, whenever they have the aptitude. At any rate, we must lead by example, so we must show them that we understand and utilize the system to our benefit.

Support "Multiculturalism" in Literature

Many people have asked this author what difference it makes for us to promote multiculturalism in the classroom and in the American and other societies. They argue that people are people and that it shouldn't be important to "separate" ourselves from the larger community with this multicultural "crap." This argument is supported by "conservatives", and other racists, who seem to be afraid of a threat to the *status quo*. The reply is that if I, and my race, are so important in the scheme of things, our discussion of race would not have been necessary. The society would have allowed us all of the opportunities and the recognition afforded to the "majority" population, without regard to creed, color, or socio-economic status. That is not the case, and so we are forced to engage in this dialogue and information gathering to "prove our contribution and our worth" to those who would believe, and have us believe, that we are inferior.

As research has been done and new information about the Africans' rich heritage is gathered, we are more and more being accused of creating "revisionist" history. How ironic that "Europeans" accuse others of revising history, when it is they who destroyed the libraries at Alexandria in Egypt, shot off the nose of the Sphinx, and are now recreating King Tut as European, etc. They are now rewriting textbooks to change even recent history.

It is these same people who have failed to figure out how the Egyptians and other Africans built the pyramids and concluded that aliens appeared from outer space, built the pyramids, then returned to their home planet(s). Or are they still here?

It is Europeans who recreated Jesus as White, even though the earliest "portraits" of Him present

Him as Black, as does the Bible. Is it that they cannot worship an African Jesus?

With the foregoing information in mind, it is important, and appropriate, that we do our own research, and present our own historical facts about Africans, on the continent and the diaspora. That is our right and our obligation. What's more, it is good for the world to know the truth about history and that people learn to respect one another for the contributions that each group has made.

Revising and updating of the literature is one of the very important means of telling the true story.

By the same token, it is important that we set up the means to disseminate the story. To that end, we need to support our historians, publishers, bookstores, libraries, and other distributors and disseminators of the literature. And we need to get the information into the classrooms, so that our students, as well as other students, will be properly educated to the truths and not just the "facts."

Community control of our education system is the key to change. I mean a change for the better, not a change for the sake of change as present-day politicians, and others, practice in these times.

Black children can be educated. The naysayers need only to look at the work of Geoffrey Canada, in Harlem, U.S.A., as well as the work of many other committed educators throughout the country.

Summary

For many years I had lambasted W. E. B. DuBois for being elitist with his theory of the "talented tenth." This posture on my part was mostly due to my conclusion of the character and actions of the man, especially in his first half century of his life.

He, I think, was jealous of and disdained Booker T. Washington because he believed that this "uneducated" upstart ex-slave had usurped his "right" to leadership of the newly-freed "colored" people. I'm not even sure whether he would consider Booker T. Washington to be one of the talented tenth. I have not seen any evidence that he did. But here he was, a Harvard-educated Negro with a Ph.D. degree and numerous academic accolades, and the uneducated, "lost-in-the-woods" folk would not recognize his leadership.

He was at odds with Washington, also, because he believed that the path to true negro liberation and success was academic education while Booker T. believed that the saving spirit rested in securing a marketable trade.

DuBois was sure that he was the heir-apparent and that once Booker T. Washington was securely in heaven he would don the mantle of leadership, but he was wrong. In from Jamaica, West Indies, strode this "rough-at-the-gills" usurper named Marcus Garvey to upend him.

He seemed to have hated Marcus Garvey passionately. From the very beginning, he sought to undermine him, but Garvey had the charisma, the vision and the support of the masses. How, then, could he be removed. DuBois conspired with the U.S. government to destroy Garvey and, after many attempts to oust him, they finally used the accusation of tax improprieties to arrest and imprison him.

The backlash of the DuBois involvement in the Garvey fiasco further crippled him in the grassroots community and precluded his rise to the helm of the movement, although he remained active in it—both nationally and internationally—all of his life.

The idea of the talented tenth, however, lives on and has now gained some credibility with me. This idea, though, can be used to include or exclude. I think DuBois mostly meant it as a tool for drawing a secure boundary around the elite, but it can be used as a clarion call for those of us who are talented to call forth that talent in service to those who are less endowed.

My involvement in the political and civic arenas over the past twenty-plus years has shown me that what is lacking—more than anything else in the African American community—is leadership. There is latent talent, galore, but our leaders, at all levels, are for the most part co-opted. They have been paid off or killed off. Those who could not be bought off with petty lower-management jobs (with no authority) have been framed and imprisoned or shot down like mongrels by the "authorities." The few remaining would-be leaders are running scared because the followers don't "have their backs."

Another problem is that those who would profess to lead are always bickering with one another—each wanting to be the "one monkey." That has to stop! We must realize that there is room for all thoughts and actions, as long as they are well thought-through and properly coordinated. We ought to realize that we must attack our dilemma from all sides, in order to conquer the blight that has us reeling, with no secure direction.

Of course, sad as it is for me to say, we must leave some people behind! There are some who cannot change, and so they become "dead weight." There are some others who are enemies within, and we must also excise those cancers. We must treat the situation we are in like that of a sinking ship. Only that which is essential for the journey must remain. Excess baggage must be thrown overboard. But, lest the elitist ones amongst us seize the moment to justify saving only themselves, let me quickly add that it is the skill of the crew, under able leadership, which will save the vessel. The officers cannot do it alone. The Talented Tenth need the skills of eighty percent to survive. One-tenth must be—and will be—discarded.

I hope that I won't be misunderstood to say that we should fail to help those who are helpless or to protect those who are infirmed or to neglect the poor, or any such scenario. We have an obligation to help those unfortunate souls who are not capable of helping themselves. The ten percent who are to be abandoned are those people who will remain albatrosses around our necks. They include those persons who disable themselves by blaming others rather than take advantage of their opportunities, however limited.

Also those people who would sell us out for "thirty pieces of silver"; those who would destroy our community with drugs and other illicit substances; those who would steal from us or murder or maim us; and, among others, those who would envy us and retard our progress.

If one is to be successful, at anything, it is important for one to study and emulate people who are, themselves, successful. It is, therefore, important for us to look at, and listen to, some of the following successful people.

Oprah Winfrey. Oprah Winfrey has been previously mentioned in this book, but her example needs repeating and expanding. There is no doubt that she is the all-time Queen of talk show. She has proved that year after year because, in spite of the fact that she is a woman and an African American, she has "blown" the competition away. It is she whom little girls want to be like, whether they are Black or White, and it is her show that women of all complexions run home to watch in the 1990s and early 2000s. Yet she has her detractors in both "communities." There are those in the White community who are jealous and hate her for her success because she is Black and those in the Black community who call her an oreo because she seems to "cotton up" to White people too much, "and neglect Black people." Some even accuse her of loving White folks and helping them while hating her own and neglecting them.

While this author cannot speak to Oprah's mind, my observation is that we in the Black community speak about power and accomplishment and about controlling our own destiny, and Oprah is the closest to doing that of any Black person who comes to mind, except for President Obama. We say we want success and we should strive to have it, yet we are always suspicious of those amongst us who attain it. We must judge people on what they do with their success instead of how they got it.

Oprah Winfrey is an example of what some of us can attain if we put our minds to it, plan it properly and work hard at it. Her success did not come from wishing and hoping, thinking and dreaming. At a glance one can see that she put the building blocks to her success firmly in place. She first had a dream. Then she looked for people who had had similar dreams to see what they had done. Next she sought opportunities and explored them. After that she looked at the horizon to see what other opportunities were available and what needs were available to be filled.

The resources to make her dreams a reality had to be identified and tapped into and the right people had to be brought into her orbit. The audience had to be brought into the mix and made comfortable and supportive. In short, she did her homework and profited from her genius and her hard work. She deserves whatever she has earned and we should value her as a role model and emulate her.

With respect to her inner being, I will repeat that I do not know how she thinks, as a person, and whether she loves White people, but her actions are of a person who loves Black people (also). She has always supported Black girls (and others) by giving scholarships. She funds programs which have helped innumerable youngsters to have a little better experience and, as the records show, she has "adopted" hundreds of AIDS children in South Africa and spends a large amount of her time fund-raising and otherwise helping these unfortunate souls. This is the measure of a human being, and she has passed with flying colors. To top it off, she has built a school in South Africa to train girls in leadership.

But for the fact that she has been able to garner the audience of large numbers of White women who boost her ratings and make the sponsors cough up big bucks to be mentioned on her show, she would not have had the financial wherewithal to pay for all of her charitable work. And her show might have been off the air.

The dollar is green, not black or white and racists have not excluded us when they are faced with earning it from us. Likewise, we must have no hesitation in nudging it from theirs and other hands. We need the dollar in order to raise ourselves from the basement! And she has been one beacon to show us how. Praise her and learn from her.

Muhammad Ali. When Muhammad Ali called himself "the Greatest" he knew of what he spoke. He was willing to put his money where his mouth was in more ways than one. He sacrificed his world heavyweight boxing championship for his belief that the Vietnam War was wrong; that the people of Vietnam had not caused him any harm; and that the United States government had denied Black Americans our civil rights at home while sending us to kill Vietnamese in the name of freedom.

Muhammad Ali did not worry that he had become one of the most hated men by White

America or that J. Edgar Hoover, the FBI chief, had branded him a public enemy. He did not worry about how many millions of dollars he would lose or the fact that he might have ended up in prison. His only concern was that he followed his conscience and stood up for what he believed in. He was a stalwart in the civil rights movement and gained converts for the cause in the White community.

He later became the most well-known and one of the most loved men in the world and his detractors have been put to shame.

Ossie Davis and ***Ruby Dee*** are the "first couple" of the civil rights movement. Although they are not touted in the history books, their contribution to the uplifting of the race is immeasurable.

This couple was often observed at the side of "famous" civil rights workers, but their contributions are, for the most part unrecognized. They have sacrificed many millions of dollars of potential earnings to help the cause, as well as contributing from their own coffers. They have given many thousands of hours speaking to people, helping people, including some in their acting profession, to be better prepared and able to find success; and they have been a double-beacon of hope to many others who wavered under the stresses of tyranny and deprivation. And, even though Ossie has gone to "his Maker", Ruby has continued, in her advanced years, to work tirelessly to improve the life of Africans, at home and throughout the diaspora. They should be saluted and emulated!

Bill Cosby. Bill Cosby has been criticized by some, and even ostracized by others, because he dared to make the observation that there are some brothers and sisters who play the blame game rather than getting off their fat asses and trying to help themselves. Is he right? Should he have said it only in private, as some of his critics have claimed he should? Does he have the right to criticize at all? The answers vary, depending on who is asked the question. So, I will put my two cents in, at the risk of also alienating some folk.

Bill Cosby has been there and done that. He has been poor and in the ghetto, and now he's rich and in the penthouse. So he knows what road to travel and how much petrol it takes to get there. But, more importantly, he knows what kind, and how many, passengers he has to take. And Mr. Cosby has helped many people along the way. He has contributed many millions of dollars to his *alma mater*, given thousands of hours of time marching and having fund-raising benefits to help students and others. He has, to this author's knowledge, even foregone his *honorarium* at a speaking engagement in lieu of his books being purchased from Black booksellers and given to members of his audience.

So he has earned the right to tell us that things will not change if we don't change them for ourselves, and that it is futile to sit on our back-ends and complain about what is being done to us. I, for one, applaud his many efforts, and believe that he might have been "crying in the wilderness" in vain, for so long, that it was time to use the media to jolt us from our slumber. We are now, at least, talking about it. Hopefully, it will spur a few thousands of us to action.

Bill and Melinda Gates. In thinking about the world of the African, we must always remember that, in spite of the inhumanity of most caucasians, not all of our friends have been and are Black. Throughout the four hundred years of Black slavery and oppression, there have been some stalwart humanitarians who have fought against man's brutality to other men. They number in the tens of thousands.

There have been stalwarts such as the aforementioned William Wilberforce in the British Parliament, down to John Brown who fielded an anti-slavery army and gave his life, to the present-day and people like Bill and Melinda Gates, who use their money to help all people.

Bill and Melinda Gates started their foundation many years ago and, among other things, gave one billion dollars to help educate African, Latino, and Native American students. It is not surprising that

Congress tried to destroy the Microsoft Corporation shortly after that. More recently, they have donated ten billion dollars to help fight AIDS in Africa. Their friend—second richest person in the world—Warren Buffet has also pledged approximately thirty billion dollars to the Gates Foundation (which already had more than thirty billion), so the chances are that some of that money will also be used to help people in Africa and the diaspora.

There are many other people who have helped the Black community, as examples to be emulated and/or as benefactors. A few are mentioned, with the hope that the reader will seek out others for thanks and recognition.

We ought to be grateful to people like these who support what is right, in spite of the strong opposition they face, everyday, from people who will call them names and, otherwise, seek to destroy them.

Amos Wilson's book, *Blueprint for Black Power,* is probably the most comprehensive book dealing with the power issues in the Black community. In speaking about the most significant issue between Blacks and Whites, he states:

> ... is an interactive one—one where White power, to a significant extent, arises out of certain types of social interactions between Whites and Blacks where Blacks unwittingly play a very important role in constituting and sustaining their power-

> lessness relative to Whites. White domination of Blacks—in our current social context—is primarily facilitated by the fact that Blacks think of themselves, and of reality, in terms created by the self-serving interests and perspectives imposed on them by Whites, and act on the basis of biased and false information provided them by Whites without realizing it. They therefore contribute to their own powerlessness and domination by Whites simply by thinking about themselves and reality in a manner that allows them to be subjugated. Thus, White domination of Blacks is, to a significant degree, covered-over by ideology, beliefs which Blacks have been conditioned by Whites to unwittingly accept. To this degree their domination and powerlessness is self-imposed. Blacks obscure their unnecessary domination by Whites and contribute to that domination by their own gullibility and too-ready acceptance of Euro-centric ideology and their obsequious willingness to think and act only within the confines of White-generated ideas, social definitions, relations and ethics (not often honored by Whites, themselves). Hence, the minds of Blacks are used to forge the links of their own mental chains.

We must remember that Amos Wilson is primarily a psychologist, and here he echoes and restates the admonition of Carter G. Woodson concerning the mis-education of the Negro and the prediction of Willie Lynch on the lasting effect of psychological slavery.

In his last speech, Martin Luther King, Jr. seemed to have recognized the problems with integration. He admonished his Black audience to bear in mind the importance of sticking together and supporting one another, psychologically, and otherwise. It is said:

> He also recognized the importance of supporting our own institutions. He advocated, for example, the transfer of funds from White institutions and informed his audience that his organization (the SCLC) had orchestrated such a transfer of their own funds. Such an action, he added, served both to strengthen the institutions in the Black community and to punish the White institutions for their mistreatment of the Black community.

We have discussed what our situation has been, what it is, and what we need to do, for ourselves, in order for us to succeed and to progress in a world where the odds are ever-increasing against us. We know that African Americans, as well as Africans everywhere, are exasperated by what they construe as accusations of laziness and lack of ambition for their failure to progress in this world, economically or otherwise.

We are at the bottom of the pile when it comes to surviving the gestation period; we have the most ailments; we live the least happy, successful lives; and we die five-plus years before the average White

American, not to mention peoples of other parts of the world. So ***we*** must change our lot. And, in the grand scale of things, money talks. However, in order to acquire the money, we must change our other habits. We must become more socially conscious, hold our religious leaders more accountable, vote and elect our own political leaders and put their feet to the fire (but have their back), get involved in the education of our children, and build and support our own businesses and financial institutions.

We have dealt with all these issues, but it bears repeating some of the main points.

We have been too passive a people and we allow others to take advantage of us, use us, and enslave us. Then we forgive them, turn the other cheek, and allow them to come into our communities, disrespect us, get rich and leave our communities destitute. Then they "gentrify" us out of these places where we call home and we are, once again, set adrift.

We allow a breakdown in our extended family structure because we try to emulate Europeans and their "nuclear" family structure, thereby abandoning the thread that has kept us alive through the centuries and nurtured us in our darkest hours.

We must rebuild that strength and get to the point where we are no longer afraid of our children and grand-children, nor of our neighbors and their children. We must, once again, be "our brothers' keepers."

We must reclaim our neighborhoods from the drug dealers and other criminal elements and we must no longer coddle people who are destroying our homes and our neighborhoods. We must tell them a resounding NO...!

We must monitor and demand the service for which we, as taxpayers pay, including our protection from the police who work in our neighborhoods and are our employees.

It is time to force them to stop killing us by forcing the politicians to stop them. It is in our interest to join neighborhood watch groups in order to let everyone know that we mean business, and contribute to organizations which protect human rights.

We must learn what is in our self-interest and not allow others to distract us with their "interests" to which they attach a civil rights label and tie their "rights" to ours. These band-wagoners are contributing to the derailment of our civil rights efforts and to the enhancements of their own causes.

We must adopt children who need a home and help the homeless and destitute in whatever way we can. At no time in our lifetime has there been a greater number of people in need than at this time, and a vast percentage are African people. We help ourselves when we help them.

Criminals must give up their untoward activities, if the community is to be saved. Whereas it is true that the police have wreaked havoc in our community with their cruelty, the criminal activities that they are hired to curtail must not be allowed to continue, and it is everybody's job to stop it.

The drug dealers in our community have proven their organizational and influence skills. They need to redirect those talents into starting and operating legitimate businesses. True, these businesses may be slightly less profitable, but they would not be running from the law and killing people, and they would contribute to rebuilding the community.

There are many other important things that we must do but, above all, we must get over the practice of discriminating against one another based on where we were born or the tones of our skin and the texture of our hair. We are the only people who label ourselves by where we were born rather than where our ancestry originated.

We have talked about the fact that the church has abrogated its traditional role in the African American community and that it is being robbed by the religious pimps and prostitutes, who have made it their personal "cash cow."

And we have urged a return to the championing of the cause of liberation in the Black community. The church needs to be a place of refuge and to get back to doing uplifting things for the community. For this mission we need "liberation" ministers.

First of all, the church needs to become involved in the clean-up of our neighborhoods, both in terms of crime and aesthetics. Secondly, it needs to be more active in mentoring our people, in general, and our youth, in particular. And not just in the religious aspects of life. The church needs to adopt parentless children and help needy people, as well as organize and promote "manhood" and "womanhood" rites-of-passage programs.

It needs to reach out and help educate people to find the means to power and a better life by exercising their rights to vote and selecting and electing the "right" candidates who will work for the benefit of their communities.

The church also needs to identify and link up volunteers who will teach their neighbors and friends (especially the children) so that they can be more successful citizens. It is the religious leaders who must convince their congregants of their role in building the economy of the Black community by spending some (if not most) of their money in that community and supporting Black financial institutions.

It is the church that must handle the problem of immorality in our community. But it cannot influence the congregation, as well as outsiders, in a positive way if the leaders of the church are also corrupt. It cannot be a beacon of fair-play and brotherhood if the leaders are thieves and scoundrels who speak with lying tongues. Congregants cannot be expected to be good if their leaders are encouraging "war-mongering" and deceit. If they call themselves Christians, they should be Christ-like. If they follow Muhammad, they should follow his true precepts. In fact, since "churches", by their very nature, are supposed to promote truth and goodness, then the leaders must remain true to their tenets. Nothing less will do, or these institutions cause more harm than good.

We, as a people, hurt ourselves politically. We waiver, in the political process, from disinterest, to ignorance, to frustration, to resignation, and we are, thereby, locked out of the political process.

First of all, we need to learn how the system works and understand that it is not meant to empower the masses, so we have to learn how to manipulate it so that it works for us. What's more, we must educate our children, from their earliest stages, about the importance of learning the political system and voting, as soon as they qualify. Furthermore, we must always have our children accompany us when we vote in all elections.

Candidates must be carefully selected, based on the short-term, as well as the long-term implications for the community, and the nation. The Party "Platform" is usually more important than the individual candidate's belief or qualification. We must look at the impact a winning candidate will have on the overall strength of a party and the ability to carry out their mandate. For example, if the party's goal is to limit one's access to health care and health care is important to you, it is important not to vote to elect Joe Blow, who is a member of that party even though he might not fully support that agenda. His election may be the cause of the Party's obtaining a majority of the seats in the "body" and being able to pass its agenda items.

One must scrutinize the history of the individual and the party and then make an "informed" selection from amongst the candidates.

Question why an individual or a party is "reaching out" to you and to other voters. They may not have an interest in you, but only in winning. And, after a candidate has been elected, don't be afraid to make a change if he/she is not performing up to par. Above all, remember that the election of a candidate should not be to the benefit of any individual, but rather to the community!

The main thesis of this book is economic development and economic quasi-independence. As was previously stated, no Black person can ever do anything from which White persons do not benefit. Therefore, we cannot ever have total economic independence.

However, we can benefit, somewhat, from the fruits of our labor if we adhere to most of the following guidelines:

Learn how the economic system works. Remember that the poor are poor because they are poor. Banks don't lend to people who cannot pay back the loan, so we must use guile and cooperation, in addition to hard work and preparation, to build our wealth. We cannot do it by anger, envy or wishing and hoping.

We must begin by saving approximately fifteen percent of our income (in Black banks). Form investment clubs and work with others to strengthen your buying power. Buy land and other real property.

It is important to train youth in business theory and practice, as well as computer and other relevant operations. It is not enough to tell them to go to a good school and get a "good" job. They must be taught to dress for success, and treat each job and situation as a training exercise for their own business operation.

We must spend at least ten percent of our money with African American enterprises and hire from the community when we are entrepreneurs.

Stellar examples of that is the authors of the book, *Prime Time,* who select Black booksellers in the different cities to provide their books, whenever they speak at conferences or gatherings. The National Black MBA Association and a couple of other organizations also use Black vendors to sell their members' books at their conventions.

We must identify and boycott racist enterprises and individuals, and not reward them with our business. We need to learn the value of the adopt-a-business concept and to practice it. It is true that there are some less-than-stellar businesspersons among us, and we need to weed them out so that the "good" ones can thrive. We need to adopt the principle of "Pay-It-Forward" whereby we support individuals with the expectations that they, in turn, support others, and continue the chain.

And, although this is a controversial issue, we need to agitate for reparations, even though we should not factor it into our decision-making and our drive for success.

Above all, we should learn and practice the Nguzo Saba (the Seven Principles of Kwanzaa) and, if we do, we will be overwhelmed with our level of financial success.

We must recognize that all the things we seek to accomplish are not do-able unless we pay attention to the main necessity for success. Education! Nothing can be accomplished until and unless we educate ourselves, as well as our children.

We must realize that education begins and ends at home. The parent and others in our community have the responsibility of educating our children and we must not abrogate our responsibilities and leave their education to outsiders who do not have our interests at heart.

We must get involved in the school system and help to formulate the curriculum and the agenda; and be advocates for public education, instead of declaring it dead and paying for our children's education in private schools. Only a few of us can afford that.

We need to demand government funding at the appropriate levels at all district schools and that funds not be siphoned off for privatization. We should not be caught up in the "no child left behind" razzmatazz and believe the hype that our children will all benefit from that sort of program. Very few will. We should not support the Faith-based initiative in education. The "Founding Fathers" were wise in their separation of church and state concept. There are just too many religions and each person supports his/her own to the exclusion of others. School should be a neutral zone.

Parents should not see good educators as the enemy, but should support the good ones and weed out the bad and we should contribute both time and money to making sure our children are properly prepared to function at a high level in this uncaring, racist world. We must all find ways to help children excel and be successful. Educated, confident children become successful, confident adults.

It is not by accident that Black people suffer from post-traumatic stress disorder. We are under constant stress in all aspects of our lives and this condition causes a deterioration of both our physical and mental health. That is why we have a lifespan of more than five years shorter than White folks. We are reminded everyday that racism is alive and well so, even though there are some persons of other ethnic groups who are not racist, they are few and far between, so we have to learn to do for ourselves.

We cannot ask the slave master to free us. We have to free ourselves and we have to build and develop our own community. We have to learn to do things in our own best interest.

In spite of our continued effort to thwart the evil of racism, it keeps rearing its ugly head and will not allow us a respite. Forty-plus years after the assassination of Martin Luther King, Jr., and all those civil rights martyrs, we find the ogre of racism still plaguing us. For those of us who might have napped in the belief that we had conquered the evil, it has reasserted itself in national attention with the case of the Jeno Six in Louisiana, in late 2007, as well as elsewhere, with increased frequency. We still find racist prosecutors and other law enforcement personnel who are unabashedly unafraid to "enforce" laws against us that are not extended to the White population. It is the reason that we must continue our battle for equality, on all levels.

The Million Man March of 1996 was a step in the right direction for the Black Community. In spite of its unseen long-term effect, we were able to get Black men, of many stripes, to recognize the value of coming together and committing to change the community for the better. The powers-that-be took praise for a subsequent reduction in crime in the community, but that commitment, I believe, was the primary reason for that effect. We need to have that gathering every ten years and recommit to cleaning up and strengthening our community.

We must realize that we are at war for our survival and so we must set up our survival mechanism as if we are forming a military organization. The church may be the Army; our educators are the Marines; the advocacy organizations are the Navy; the businesspersons are the Air Force; and the civil rights organizations would constitute to Coast Guard. They would all have their own leader, but would have to operate as a joint unit with a

Chairman of the Joint Chiefs of Staff. This would eliminate the competition which we now find amongst our organizations, with each vying for sole recognition, while "spinning their wheels."

There are those amongst us who have lost hope for any improvement in our lot as a people and there are some who blame our condition on us. Whatever the circumstances or wherever the blame, one must conclude that this condition cannot be allowed to prevail.

We, the victims are the only ones with a vested interest in changing the condition. So, we must recognize encumbrances to our progress and neutralize them. We must also recognize the opportunities which either present themselves or the ones we can seize to turn the tide of distress to the tranquil sea of success. It won't be easy.

We must not be dissuaded by those neo-fascists and hate-mongers who still, in 2010, chase the trend of hanging nooses to frighten us. May they be damned!

I am chagrined about how few Black people realize how tenuous our lot really is and who are willing to do something to improve the race. I am, though, encouraged by the number of young Black people who are conscious of their responsibility to positively represent the race, and to scale any hurdle they find in their way. They are proud of their heritage and who they are.

I am also encouraged that, although racism is rampant throughout the world, there are still many "Europeans" (and others) who don't seem to recognize color or creed in their dealing with other people. Such was my experience in recent visits to Ipswich, England. It is also my experience with my White next-door neighbor, who turns out to be the best neighbor I have ever had.

There are many who tell us that, with the election of Barack Obama, we have entered the post-racial period. I am one of the happiest people in the world over the election of President Obama, but I cannot emphasize too much that his election alone does not change the hatred in people's heart.

If anything, the hate-mongers are strengthening their resolve to destroy people who don't look like and are not part of "them." Just look at the "tea-party" people, and others, who are fighting like a bunch of mad dogs to shift power solely to themselves. They are running scared that they will lose their perceived God-given sense of superiority as others realize the lie that we have been fed these thousands of years as Europeans have changed the history books. They are attempting to overtly do that again, in Texas, where they are modifying the textbooks and not allowing ethnic studies. Other states are following suit.

We must realize that we are not facing only race hatred. People seem to be extremely mean and selfish in these times of hardship. In July, 2010, there was, in Texas, the case of this family who lost their home to the callousness of a Home Owners Association. They failed to pay the association dues of approximately $977.00. The homeowners' association sold their $300,000.00+ home for $3,201.00 to someone who resold it for $135,000.000.

There was a hullabaloo about it only because of the question of whether the husband was on active military duty at the time of the transaction. What impressed me the most, however, were readers' responses on the internet. It ranged from people blaming the wife for not paying the bills and, therefore justifying the association's actions, to asserting that if they could not afford to pay the bills they should not live there, to they should not lose it because the husband is in the military.

Of the more than one hundred responses that I read, very few, indeed, considered the fact that the penalty did not fit the crime and that the association had no justification for selling the people's house for $3,201.00, or about one percent of value. They had other alternatives such as putting a lien on the property so that it could not be sold without paying the dues. Where is the mercy? Where is the humanity, both from the association and the people responding to the article? There is none.

The election of Obama means that we have a beacon of hope of a bright future <u>if we seize the</u>

opportunity to work together and build up ourselves and our nation. We have not received a free ride. As a matter of fact, President Obama cannot do for us, in the short term, as much as a white president of good will could, because all eyes are on him, looking to see and to condemn him for any presumed favoritism toward any persons of color, let alone African Americans.

The problems of the world, especially as it relates to racism, are too complex to be solved by one person or one book. Suffice it to say, if we follow the premises which are postulated in this book (along with other ideas which other people may have) we will go a long way to making our lives much more bearable and pleasant.

At any rate, those of us who recognize what needs to be done to help our race must continue to cry in the wilderness while we take the hands of our young people and show them the way to the salvation of our race (and benefit to the world).

We should diligently seek peace and brotherhood with all races, at all times, but we must have that relationship as equals. We must not sit at the shared table as beggars but as negotiators and fellow decision-makers. Anything less is unacceptable. But only we can make that happen, by our thoughts and actions. Ultimately, change is in our hands!

References

----------- "The First Black Power Town." *Ebony*, Vol. XXVII, No. 4, Feb., 1972.

----------- "Suggesting Apology for Slavery Draws Hate Mail." *The Final Call*, Vol. 16, No. 40, August 5, 1997.

----------- *Let's Make a Slave.* The Black Liberation Library, 1970.

Armah, Ayi Kwei, *Two Thousand Seasons.* Reading, England: Heinemann, 1973.

Associated Press, "Ideology of Hate Behind Church Fires, Group Says." Rock Hill, SC *Herald,* Mar 12, 1997.

Baker, Ray Stannard, *Following Color Line: American Negro Citizenship in Progressive Era.* New York: Doubleday, Page, 1908.

Bonura, Chris, "Business Capital Urged Blacks—NAACP President Vows Fight in BR Speech." Baton Rouge, LA *Advocate*, Mar. 30, 1997.

Bradley, Ed, Tulia, TX. *60 Minutes*, September 28, 2003.

Brown, Tony, *Black Lies, White Lies: The Truth According to Tony Brown.* New York: Quill/William Morrow, 1995.

Buggs, Shannon, "No Conspiracy in Church Burnings, State Report Says Task Force Finds Race Relations Remain a Problem." Raleigh, NC *News & Observer*, June 19, 1997.

Canada, Geoffrey, *Fist, Stick, Knife, Gun: A Personal History of Violence in America.* Boston: Beacon Press, 1995.

Carew, Jan, *Rape of Paradise: Columbus and the Birth of Racism in the Americas.* New York: Seaburn Publishing, 2006.

Chappell, Kevin, "What's Behind the Burning of Black Churches." *Ebony*, Sept., 1996.

Clinton, William J., "Remarks to the Women's Int'l Convention of the Church of God in Christ in New Orleans, Louisiana." *Weekly Compilation of Presidential Documents*, June 3, 1996.

Courtney, Brian, "Penalties Called Key to Stopping Hate Crimes." Knoxville *News Sentinel,* Dec. 6, 1996.

Fierce, Milfred C., *Slavery Revisited: Blacks and the Southern Convict Lease System, 1865-1933.* New York: Africana Studies Research Center, Brooklyn College, 1994.

Ford, Glen, "Study Shows Blacks Will Never Gain Wealth Parity with Whites Under Current System." *Black Agenda Report,* May 19, 2010.

Franklin, John Hope, and Moss, Alfred A., Jr., *From Slavery to Freedom: A History of Negro Americans.* New York: McGraw-Hill, Inc., 1988.

Gaston, Marilyn & Porter, Gayle, *Prime Time.* New York: Random House, 2001.

Gibbons, Don C., "Review Essay: Race, Ethnicity, Crime, and Social Policy." *Crime and Delinquency,* Jul., 1997.

Greene, David L., "Clergy Group Backing Pastor in Fire Case Here. Delegation Will Visit, Question Officials." *St. Louis Post-Dispatch,* Aug. 8, 1997.

Howard, Peter E., & Barry, Rick, "Lyons Backers Point Fingers at Other Groups." *American Business Review,* Sept. 20, 1997.

James, Joy, *Transcending the Talented Tenth.* New York: Routledge, 1997.

Kimbro, Dennis & Hill, Napoleon, *Think and Grow Rich: A Black Choice.* New York: Fawcett Crest, 1991.

Leno, Jay. *The Tonight Show,* NBC Television.

Lokeman, Rhonda Chriss, "Talking About Race Is National Obsession." *Kansas City Star,* June 22, 1997.

Pleasant, Betty, "Bottom Line: Witness to Killing Fears Cover-Up in Execution of African American Suspect." *Los Angeles Wave,* April 28, 2010.

Shah, Ali, "Authorities Investigating Fire at Minnesota's First Black Church." *Star Tribune,* Jul. 15, 1997.

Slevin, Peter & Cannon, Angie, "150 Church Fires Solved." *American Business Review,* June 9, 1997.

Smith, R. C., "Prince Edward County: Revisited and Revitalized." *The Virginia Quarterly Review,* Winter, 1997.

Thomas, Robert McG., Jr., "George W. Crockett Jr., House Member, Civil Rights Champion." *Pittsburgh Post-Gazette*, Sept. 16, 1997.

Towns, Hollis R., "Church Fires Study Finds 'Conspiracy'." *The Atlanta Journal*, Mar. 12, 1997.

Walker, Robin, *When We Ruled*. London: Every Generation Media, 2006.

Wesseling, H. L., *Divide and Rule: Partition of Africa, 1880-1914*. Translated, Arnold J. Pomerans. Connecticut: Praeger, 1996.

Wilson, Amos, *Blueprint for Black Power*. New York: Afrikan World InfoSystems, 1998.

Wilson, Charles Reagan, "Church Burnings and the Black Community." *The Christian Century*, Sept. 25-Oct. 2, 1996.

Woodson, Carter G., *The Miseducation of the Negro*. Washington, DC: The Associated Publishers, Inc., 1933.

Zinn, Howard, *People's History of the United States: 1492-Present*. New York: HarperPerennial, 1980, 2003.